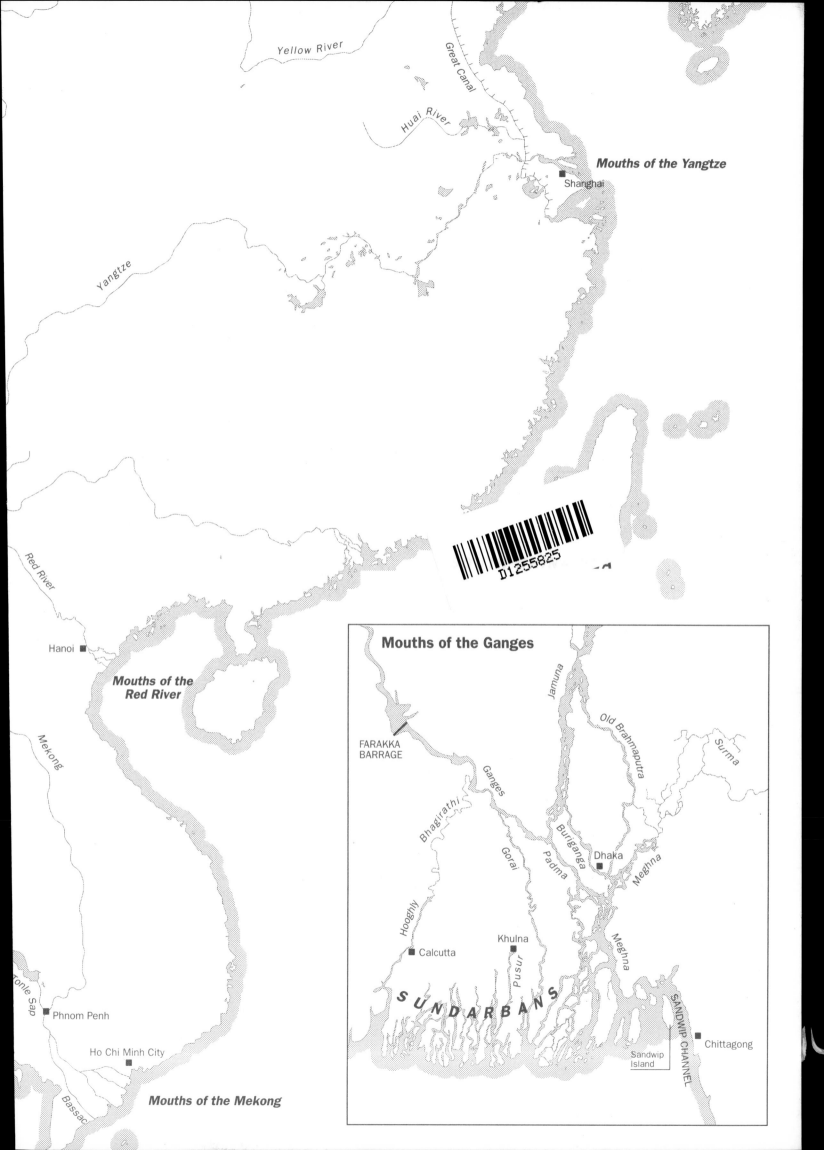

Yellow River

Great Canal

Huai River

Mouths of the Yangtze

■ Shanghai

Yangtze

Red River

Hanoi ■

**Mouths of the
Red River**

Mekong

D1255825

Mouths of the Ganges

Jamuna

Old Brahmaputra

Surma

FARAKKA
BARRAGE

Bhagirathi

Ganges

Goral

Buriganga

Padma

Dhaka ■

Meghna

Hooghly

Khulna ■

Pusur

Meghna

SANDWIP CHANNEL

■ Calcutta

S U N D A R B A N S

Sandwip
Island

■ Chittagong

Tonle Sap

Phnom Penh ■

Ho Chi Minh City ■

Bassac

Mouths of the Mekong

Delta

Daniel Schwartz

Delta

The Perils, Profits and Politics of Water in South and Southeast Asia

Introduction by Tim Page

With 163 photographs in duotone

Thames and Hudson

Captions translated from the German
by Lorna Dale

British Library Cataloguing-in-Publication Data

A catalogue record for this book is available from
the British Library

ISBN 0-500-01753-0

Printed and bound in Germany by Steidl, Göttingen

On the half title: Going home across the Padma.
Sibchar, Madaripur District, Bangladesh.

River mouths

The Brahmaputra, which rises in Tibet and flows through
the Indian state of Assam, becomes the Jamuna when
it enters Bangladesh and after it meets the Ganges the
two rivers flow towards the sea, first as the Padma and
then as the Meghna – named after the big feeder river
from the Sylhet basin. The body of water, which
eventually flows into the Gulf of Bengal over an area
up to 20 kilometres wide, is the second largest delta
in the world after the Amazon.

On the title page: Rainy season over Kompong Chhnang
Province, Cambodia.

The taming of the Mekong

The Tonle Sap, the Great Lake, is the lungs of
Cambodia. In the monsoon season from June to
October the swollen Mekong forces back the water
flowing out of the lake. The lake doubles in size
and irrigates the central rice-growing areas to the
south of Angkor.

Hydroelectric projects are now endangering this
unique phenomenon, which plays a vital part in the
hydrology of the Lower Mekong Basin. They are based
on a grandiose plan to use the last untamed river in
the world, which comes from China, flows through
Laos and Cambodia and pours into the South China
Sea in Vietnam. The hydroelectric projects originated
from the domino theory of the early sixties, when Asia
had to be protected against the advance of communism;
however, they did not come to fruition because of the
second Indochinese war and the conflict in Cambodia.

In the process of sustainable development many
of the projects were cancelled or modified, but at the
same time others were planned or built to supply the
fast-growing Southeast Asian economy with cheap
energy. The needs of the neighbouring countries
had changed.

Laos, through which the Mekong flows for one-third
of its total length of 4,200 kilometres and where almost
half its tributaries rise, has little to export apart from
water power and it is anxious to play a central role in
international discussions. Thailand is seeking political
support from Burma and China, the countries in the
upper reaches of the Mekong in need of electricity,
to use water from the river for its rice-growing areas.
Vietnam, the last country through which the river passes,
needs enormous quantities of river water to feed its
irrigation canals and counteract the penetration of salty
seawater and it fears for the ecological balance in its
rice-growing area in the delta if the use of the Mekong
is extended.

Contents

Captions to preceding pages

Pages 6/7: Boatman in Shuiyang, Anhui Province, China.

The river in wartime

People began building dams in China in the period of the Warring States (481–221 BC), when human sacrifices still appeased the river gods and were believed to prevent floods. Over the centuries the dams constantly had to be raised as massive loess deposits built up on the bottom of the river bed until eventually it was above the level of the surrounding land. Dams became instruments of war.

In the face of death and destruction Confucius (551–479 BC), on his wanderings in the Chinese heartland between the Yangtze and the Yellow River, is supposed to have urged the warring princes to enter into pacts which controlled the strategic breaching of dams.

In 1938 the Nationalist troops again used the Yangtze, the 'Long River', as a weapon and destroyed dams to halt the Japanese advance in the hinterland of Shanghai, the Yangtze Delta, a lakeland area.

Page 8: Shipyard worker in the bowels of a Russian freighter. Haiphong, Vietnam.

Riverroads

Between 1866 and 1868 a French expedition, spurred into action by British advances up the Salween and Irrawaddy rivers in Burma, explored the course of the Mekong. However, sandbanks and rapids destroyed the illusion that a navigable trade route could be opened up for the French colony of Cochin China (now in southern Vietnam) from Saigon to the Chinese province of Yunnan, a rich source of tea and silk.

The expedition discovered the Red River, which flows into the Gulf of Tonkin. The port of Haiphong, the gateway to Hanoi and its delta, was captured in 1873. It became the northern base for French colonization, which did not end until 1954.

Page 10: Jute mats being unloaded in the harbour on the Tonle Sap. Phnom Penh, Cambodia.

Lifeline

At the end of 1974 the Khmer Rouge were at the gates of Phnom Penh; all road links to the capital were broken off. The Mekong and its tributary the Bassac were the only lifelines, on which barques brought rice, fuel and ammunition from the delta to the beleaguered capital. The convoys were at constant risk of ambush. With the onset of the dry season, the shipping channels became narrower and traffic was halted completely when mines attached to small bamboo rafts were deployed. Phnom Penh fell on 17 April 1975.

The Vietnamese troops, which drove Pol Pot into the jungle four years later, in January 1979, found the capital empty. *Angkar Padevat*, the Revolutionary Organization of Democratic Kampuchea, had evacuated all the town centres; their inhabitants died in the notorious killing fields or fled to Thailand. Ships lay sunk in Phnom Penh harbour. The bridge across the Tonle Sap between the harbour and its confluence with the Mekong was blown up.

In 1994 the bridge was restored. There are plans to build a new harbour. But as long as the political uncertainty continues, larger ships with a higher registered tonnage, which should be linking Cambodia to the region's thriving economic centres, remain a dream.

The wooden barques that put in there today bring rice, tobacco and other goods from the 'Great Lake' – also known as Tonle Sap – or take on passengers for the journey up the Mekong to the Laotian border or out to sea towards Vietnam.

Pages 12/13: On board the *Withaka*. Twante Canal, Burma.

Rulers in the Golden Land

British warships and troop transporters first sailed up the Irrawaddy as far as Mandalay, the royal city in Upper Burma, in 1824; Lower Burma was annexed in 1852. The ships the East India Company had provided for the war – four freight steamers and dozens of sailing barques – were taken over by the Scottish Irrawaddy Flotilla Company in 1856. After the whole of Burma was annexed in 1885 the company also sailed the upper reaches of the Irrawaddy and the Chindwin; in the 1930s it owned more than 600 ships and had a monopoly of passenger and goods transport.

Oil came to Rangoon from the fields in the middle reaches of the Irrawaddy, as did salt from the delta. Hundreds of kilometres upstream, the rafts with their cargo of wood began their trip to the sawmills in the capital, a journey that could take weeks.

In the 1960s precious woods replaced rice as the biggest foreign-currency earner. But by that time 'Burma's Road to Socialism' had already become the road to poverty. The old-style despotism spread fear and shut the country off from the rest of the world.

Introduction

The great rivers are somehow romantic claws in our minds. They represent the famed voyages of adventure and discovery. They appeal to the Tom Sawyer, the Huck Finn, the *Wind in the Willows* Ratty in our desire to mess about in boats in situations that do not seem absurdly fraught with danger – to float nostalgically down a wide stream from source through confluence to estuary. The larger rivers, those that have shaped the face of the planet, usually end up with deltas lazed across vast tracts of land liable to instant flood and destruction.

Most exploratory travels have started at these deltas. They are the font of the unfurling of the hinterland, of man's conquest of the surface of his world. Modern tourism, coupled with the ebb and flow of wars and the communication of them to the rest of the globe by geometrically progressing, now digitalized, media, has paled the original conquests and derring-do of centuries ago. Today, we arrive in these once exotic locales to be met by tour groups of video-toting Japanese, French doctors or gawking backpackers. Our world is now miniaturized, sterilized for package consumption, the realities sanitized out so as not to offend our carefree attitude toward the harshness that abounds. To our minds, it is radically chic to be confronted by the starkness in a television documentary broadcast at an hour when the children are safely tucked up in bed, or to catch a glimpse of something serious in that shrinking portion of a magazine that is sandwiched between ever more insistent exhortations to consume. The prevailing attitude now is one of purchase begets happiness. We seem to have lost our focal points, our awareness of our world. It has all become too distant for serious contemplation unless it is enveloped in our holiday destination. We are less spiritual, our morality is on a decline, and we seem unable to glean from a Siddharthic perception. Now there is rarely a slow journey to the East – we are propelled there by Boeing and Rolls Royce, untouched by even the remotest acquaintance with a large percentage of the world's population.

Daniel has focused closely in on these labyrinths, immersed himself and his Hasselblad in the intricate waterways of the most magnetic regions of the Asian continent.

Asia will always be quixotic. We as westerners will never quite grasp the inner rationales of the Orient: the philosophic instead of the dogmatic. The tantric yin and yang spin eludes our societies caught in a web of economic preoccupation.

Admittedly, Asia too is fast drifting in that direction, the gods changing from Buddha, Tao and Confucius to Daewoo, Sony and Honda.

Communism has withered on its vine, replaced by 'free' market economies. Stoic, deep-rooted, socialist nationalist parties have mellowed to accommodate the new neocolonialisms – the invasion of the international mega-corporations, those giants of conformity who would have us consume the same burger, drink the same soft drink or drive an identical vehicle on a global scale; the same hydras who do not deign to see it of tantamount interest to invest in a policy of environmental concern or ecological renovation. In the race for profits, humanity and its condition are disregarded.

We in England are accustomed to nice, placid, meandering rivers and drooping deciduous trees, an idyllic concept confounded only by the presence of downstream docks and ports. Ours is a pastoral concept that leaves us bereft when faced with the sheer immensity of the great streams of the world. The Ganges and the Mekong are up there among the top five biggies. The Irrawaddy, the Brahmaputra, the Red River also rank high. A great percentage of South and Southeast Asia's populace lives directly beside or derives its livelihood from them. Downstream the rivers are miles across – seemingly lakes or seas. They are tropical; also alien, fetid and fecund. They are no longer the lame *Wind in the Willows* theme; they have become dragons, friend or foe dependent on seasonal mood swings. There always appears to be an endless sea of vaguely unattractive mud abounding in them, mud you know would eat you alive, that is itself alive, bubbling, gurgling, reproducing and spawning flora and fauna familiar from the pages of *National Geographic*. Up close, the rivers take on a different patina, one that

commands respect. Crossing them is ever daunting. Even when there is a sizeable span, it seems to become a funnel of humanity; fords are something shallow, somewhere upstream, and not in the wet season; ferries constitute the most photographic focal points anywhere. On these giant swirling currents of the Orient, any ferry crossing could reduce you to two column inches in a broadsheet newsprint as one of those small items of a 'collapse, roll over, swamping, missing, presumed dead' disaster that merit no more than cursory attention. When you are a local, they are timeless tragedies which unfold with monotonous regularity – the price of living in the underdeveloped third or fourth world. It is hard for us in our secure environment to comprehend the scale of such disasters, as though we had to come to terms with a mega commuter train crash quintupled every week or a pleasure boat packed with revellers rolled over daily. Travel in most of the underdeveloped world, the world of these floodplains, is at best haphazard. Overcrowded boats and ferries sink, many of the passengers never manifested; trains replete with roofracks full of free riders plunge from flash-flood-weakened bridges; dodgy overloaded trucks and buses veer off pot-holed highways into roadside canals. They are all anathemas to our ordered senses. To the Bengalis, Burmans, Khmer, Viet and Chinese they are the expected norm.

The spirituality of these peoples is based on the eventualities that can befall them. The spirits of the waters, the rocks, the trees must be appeased and offerings made to them. This is interwoven in the fabric of their religious or philosophical attitudes and beliefs. Fundamentalist Muslims, devout Hindus, tranquil Buddhists and outright atheists all hug on to the more ancient gods, for the force of Mother Nature stands proud in all their creeds. Devotions must be made to the waters that rule life, where existence ebbs and flows in rhythms that man can but strive to control and which sublimate him into obeyance.

The festivals observing these primordial powers, especially those of the moon, necessitate ceremonies of most intricate formulae and patterns. Merit is gained in the attendance; the very ability to continue surviving is dominated by the refreshment and faith instilled in making pilgrimages to the auspicious site of the ceremony. It is often on these pilgrimages that overcrowded transport falls foul of the gods, that natural disasters sweep in with fury, merely reinforcing the steadfastness of the religious.

The waters themselves become sacred. The holy Ganges is mother to the Hindus. Millions trek to the source, converge on Benares or descend to the multi-armed mother-goddess of its delta to be nourished from its flow. On the Irrawaddy and the Mekong, both multi-gorged, are found Chedi, Shwe, Tat and temples all established to bestow blessings on travellers endangered below. The high, dry spots in the deltaic plains usually boast ancient stupas and monasteries, becoming focal points for the surrounding populace, simple superstitious souls whose lives have been nothing but endless agrarian toil and occasional strife.

The trouble has been compounded in colonial and post-colonial times by the passage of political turmoil and sweeping wars. It started with the arrival of the European powers seeking to exploit their new dominions – firstly the Portuguese and Dutch with minor enclaves, followed by the British and French. Then from the east came the Chinese and Japanese. The only country not to suffer the indignities of colonization was the Kingdom of Siam (now Thailand), whose rulers succeeded in astutely playing off the conquerors on their borders, cosying up to the then superpowers. Around them, nascent liberation movements began to flourish. Initially successfully repressed, their leading cadres driven underground, they would eventually change the face of global geopolitics. Their strength would not be consummated until news of the demise of the participants in World War One began to waft around the tropics in the twenties and thirties. With it came the fresh breeze of communism, attempting to convince the common man to rise up in the name of a new world-wide social order. The logic of it was not lost on the repressed, indentured or enslaved workers in the mills and on the plantations the Europeans had created. The irony was that the chosen few to be educated were often the ones who martyred themselves in furthering the cause of the masses. It was an unstoppable process, interrupted only by, and then enhanced by, World War Two.

Independence sprang up as the curtain on hostilities was drawn, leaving the colonialistic Allies hungry to retake advantage of the vacuum left by the Japanese. The Japanese had envisaged a co-prosperity sphere eventually linking up with an Axis-influenced zone across the Islamic Middle East. It was not to be, but it gave a taste to the newly awakening nationalistic fronts that had become strengthened as guerrilla movements against the new oriental imperialist order. Gandhi and Jinnah were about to create a new order for a billion people. Ho Chi Minh, having come out of the jungle when the Office of Strategic Services (precursor of the CIA) declared Vietnam independent, was about to go back to the maquis once more. The Chinese were still at civil war, warlording and starving, while the Burmese question would remain a played-down British issue. Around the perimeter, other struggles against erstwhile landlords rose with cries instilled by a newfangled American-inspired democracy. Economies abetted by recovery plans started to put the vanquished back in the driver's seat; those choosing a socialistic path saw themselves marginalized and running out of gas. Strong-arm dictators and fledgling emperors found themselves installed over the destiny of millions of liberated peoples living on a subsistence level with iniquitous land tenure still in full sway. As always, the peasants bore the brunt of the forces of government and of nature.

Plunging into this modern maelstrom, the elements of history are not readily apparent. It is only with the passage of time and enlightenment that the lotus opens petal after petal to reveal the inner intricacies, the various tortuous paths that these regions conspire to offer. Herein lies one's own inner awakening. When you first catch sight of Angkor Wat or the Taj Mahal, you are at a loss to explain your emotions. The East sucks you in and digests you, leaving things to be resolved residually. When I first glimpsed the Mekong in 1963 before crossing it from Nong Kai in Thailand into Laos,

my fantasy flew to its source and to its delta in the instant and irrepressible desire to embrace them both. A majestic feeling. The Irrawaddy I followed almost illusively, first hitchhiking through bandit territory along its upper lengths and finally catching a paddle-wheeler from Mandalay to Pagan – my Kiplingesque dreams fulfilled. Now, Nile-style, yuppie-targeted, air-conditioned floating nightmares ply the stream, contravening a general embargo thrown up against the SLORC-run regime in Rangoon (now changed to Yangon, while Burma has evolved to Myanmar, with a surfeit of corrupt generals denying any democratic principals to their once-free electorate). In Cambodia the lotus is still unfolding, the light gradually penetrating the bud as the Khmer Rouge fade back to a fiefdom, leaving other tyrannical figures to corrupt a long-awaited peace. Downstream in Vietnam, the path has become radically chic and touristy. The Mekong delta is boom city with up to three crops of rice being harvested a year, promoting the Vietnamese into the top three global producer exporters. Up there with their ex-enemies the US and Thailand. ASEAN (Association of South East Asian Nations) expands to include the Viets, while the Khmer and Lao have observer status. Burma remains a policy thorn in everyone's psyche.

It is in the Mekong that Daniel finds his roots, uncovers the missing spiritual links in his own ancestry. The wave of that knowledge ripples out to the extremities that hedge the perimeter: to the north Shanghai, to the west Calcutta. Finally to return to your Vietnamese grandmother's native village must be one of the ultimate voyages of self-discovery,

Hesse's catharsis, a whole lotus ready for laying on the shrine of one's soul. Its expression, needs be, will become surreal in this strange place. It is a weird route from Switzerland to Bac Liêu; it is an odyssey that assumes freakish dimensions: each step dictated by circumstance, carefully laid plans thwarted, the eventual go-with-the-flow instinctively followed.

And much of this with a 6 x 6 Hasselblad – not the most portable piece of kit or the easiest to use in disparate conditions. Its bulky format doesn't have the robust austerity of the 35mm; its infrastructure is doubled.

Daniel has focused in on these watery labyrinths with a dour Swiss sense of technocracy coupled with an artist's misgivings and conception of the unexplored, with a freshness that beguiles you into an understanding of the profound nature of the self-search. These are oblique 'people' pictures, not the formulated, complex, composed architectural frames that consumed him for years in Greece and obsessed him in tracing the Great Wall of China. We are suddenly intimate with this gangly, long-haired man with his darting, intense, slightly oriental eyes. We see the tall calm, the maturity emerging in discovery. The approach stays structured; the frames appear composed, only to confound us in their movement, tilting the ordinary to the bizarre, becoming in this transition a surreal homage to the photographers of the thirties, his Bauhaus heritage. A Germanic sense of order prevails through the post-hip attitude gleaned from the realms of photojournalism. The latter's infiltration into this Swiss schismatic underlines the neutrality with which the images are shot. He gets caught up in the violence that threatens the fragile peace that is now emerging, confronts compassionately the catastrophes that either promote a trip or invade the calm of one half done. Schwartz seemed to pop up in strange locations – Kompong Thom, Tay Ninh, Ho Chi Minh City, Prey Veng, places that have been my territory for decades. Bumping into a friendly face in such circumstances is always auspicious. Sharing one's own addiction to the East is simply an immeasurable pleasure, making the agonies and ecstasies more acceptable, more replete. An easy kindred spirit helps to while away the hours of no light, the spaces between the imagery spasms.

It is rare that the art photographer, that outsider to the craft, turns his eye to journalism and takes to the field, to the coal-face. Werner Bischof did so, and the effect is here in these angled images surrealistically addressing the fundamental issues confronting twenty per cent of the planet's populace. While Gilles Peress approaches the subject on the surrealistic macro level, Schwartz collages the micro together with a broader brush: global minimalism, superbly printed, finest grain – all in the best Swiss tradition.

Tim Page

1

Delta in the Making

The Bengal Basin

In the Oligocene Period (38 to 26 million years ago), some time after the [Indian and Eurasian] plates collided, a portion of the northeastern part of India fractured and sank below sea-level. This portion was gradually filled up to form the eastern part of the Bengal Basin.… Due to its position, with one of the world's major subduction faults in the north and a major transform fault in the east, the Bengal Basin and its adjacent area is an active tectonic region. Large areas within Bangladesh have been uplifted in recent times and some areas are still sinking.…

The Bengal Basin has been filled by sediments washed down from the highlands on three sides of it, and especially from the Himalayas, where the slopes are steeper and the rocks less consolidated. The greater part of this land-building process must have been due to the Ganges and Brahmaputra rivers. The origin of the Ganges and Indus rivers is much debated. On the evidence of the Siwalik deposits (between 1 to 12 million years old) in the Indo-Gangetic Valley, E.H. Pascoe (1919) and G.E. Pilgrim (1919) advanced the hypothesis of an Indo-Brahm or Siwalik river flowing westward and southward to Sind and draining the vast plains. Post-Siwalik movements are said to have dismembered this river, which broke up into the Indus, Ganges and Brahmaputra.

The latter two reversed their flow and found a new course to the sea through the Garo-Rajmahal gap. This theory has been challenged (Krishnan & Aiyengar: 1940), but not seriously shaken. If accepted, it means that much of the Bengal Basin formed on the reversal of the Indo-Brahm in the late Pliocene period (7 to 25 million years ago).

Haroun er Rashid, *Geography of Bangladesh,* 2nd edn, The University Press Limited, Dhaka, 1991, p. 7.

The Immature Delta

This very low land of some 4827 sq. km area contains the Sunderban forest and the Sunderban reclaimed estates (cultivated land). There are two possible causes for the existence of such a large very low estuarine area – insufficient deposition by the Ganges distributaries or subsidence. Till the seventeenth century, the main Ganges distributary seems to have been the Hoogly-Bhagirathi. In the next century, the Ganges sent more and more water down its more eastern distributaries, till the 1787 flood and the breakthrough of the Jamuna forced it back and the Gorai distributary was enlarged.

Preceding pages: After the 1991 cyclone; returning to the scene of the disaster. Banskhali, Chattagram District, Bangladesh.

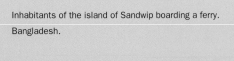

Inhabitants of the island of Sandwip boarding a ferry. Bangladesh.

The Ganges subsequently once again shifted east. Between the Hoogly-Bhagirathi and the Gorai (and its continuation – the Madhumati) the Ganges had two main distributaries, the Ichamati and the Bhairab, neither of which built up more than their own levees. The Jalangi and Mathabhanga rivers cut across the drainage lines of these rivers in the eighteenth century, but their work lasted only about a century. It seems, therefore, that the main distributaries of the Ganges never flowed through this region, and the small ones that did lasted a few centuries at most. The building up of this estuarine area is consequently not complete. The tides may have also contributed to the retardation by forcing the major part of the sediments to be deposited along the ledge, which extends from the levee of the Madhumati and Narail Upazila west-south-westwards to the Hoogly-Bhagirathi at Calcutta.

It is possible that subsidence has played a major part in depressing this area. There are many evidences of it, such as large ruins in the heart of the swampy estuarine areas such as at Shekertek and Bedkashi (Fawcus 1927), and the presence of human artifacts and tree stumps, buried in the alluvium many feet below the level of the sea. Hunter (1875) recorded the presence of large tree trunks buried in the ground at Khulna town, indicating a subsidence of 6 meters....

The sea-ward face of this region is a network of branching streams around roughly oblong shaped islands. When silt laden streams reach sea, their velocity is checked and their sediment load is flocculated. Bars form at the mouths, and the streams branch off to either side. In time these branches too form their bars and are also divided. As this process goes on the branches unite and redivide and the bars coalesce into islands, which are sometimes cut apart. This process forms a network of channels.

The high tide ponds back the estuarine rivers and force them to break their banks and open out cross-channels. These are a marked feature of the low areas much affected by tides, for 'as the delta is elevated out of tidal influence, the cross-channels disappear' (Strickland 1940).

Haroun er Rashid, *Geography of Bangladesh*, 2nd edn, The University Press Limited, Dhaka, 1991, pp. 31–32.

The Sundarbans

Sundarbans forest basically is a deltaic swamp. It occupies the southwest corner of Bangladesh between 89° 02′ E and 89° 53′ E and 21° 38′ N and 21° 29′ N along the shore of the Bay of Bengal. This sundarban forest is a very

Reception centre for flood victims. Bhangura, Bangladesh.

23

large tract of natural mangroves with approximately 580,000 ha under management out of which 177,000 ha are creeks and rivers....

The Sundarbans receives large volume of fresh water from inland rivers flowing from the north and of saline water from the twice daily tidal incursions from the sea. The relative contributions from the two sources of water are not constant through the year. The bulk of fresh water reaches the forest in the monsoon season from June to September. During the dry season, the fresh water flow decreases progressively, resulting in a prolonged saline influence which persists until the fresh water flow increases again....

The salinity of the forest floor and high monsoonic rainfall of 2,000 mm per annum dictate the composition and structure of this natural mangrove forest of Sundarbans and artificial plantation in the coastal region....

Evidence of adequate sedimentation and appearance of indicative grass, dhansi (*Oryza coarctata*), are prerequisites [for afforestation]. Keora is planted on low mudflats with low salinity and Baen, Kakra and Gewa are planted on high mudflats with higher salinity.

M.N.A. Katebi, 'Mangrove Wetlands and Forest Management in Bangladesh', in H. Isozaki, M. Ando, Y. Natori (eds), *Towards Wise Use of Asian Wetlands*, International Lake Environment Committee Foundation, Kusatsu, Japan, 1993, pp. 92, 95.

The Bay of Bengal

The Bay of Bengal is bordered on the north by the deltaic regions of the Ganges and Brahmaputra rivers, on the east the Burmese peninsula and its extension to the south the Andaman and Nicobar Ridges, the submerged continuation of the Arakan Yoma ranges, and on the west Indian peninsula and Srilanka....

It is observed that in the north and northeastern part of the Bay of Bengal, the mean sea level has an increasing tendency and in the southern part of the eastern coast of India there is a tendency of decreasing sea level keeping the constant level at Waltair. For example, the mean sea level at Rangoon was about 16 cm. in 1962 compared to the sea level in 1920. In Chittagong the mean sea level raised about 25 cm. in 1964 in comparison to the sea level of 1944. In Calcutta, sea level also raised to about 16 cm. and in Diamond Harbour 10 cm. Only in Khidirpur, the sea level remained almost constant. In the Island Sagar, the sea level raised almost 30 cm. compared to the sea level of 1931.

Subash Chandra Das, 'Physical Oceanography of the Bay of Bengal', in K. Maudood Elahi, A.H.M. Raihan Sharif, A.K.M. Abul Kalam (eds), *Bangladesh: Geography, Environment and Development*, Bangladesh National Geographical Association, Dhaka, 1992, pp. 36, 47.

Islanders looking for valuables after their houses
have disappeared into the sea. Sandwip, Bangladesh.

Sea-Level Rise

Global mean surface temperature has increased by between 0.3 and 0.6° C since the late 19th century, a change that is unlikely to be entirely natural in origin. The balance of evidence, from changes in global mean surface air temperature and from changes in geographical, seasonal and vertical patterns of atmospheric temperatures, suggests a discernible human influence on global climate. There are uncertainties in key factors, including the magnitude and patterns of long-term natural variability. Global sea level has risen by between 10 and 25 cm over the past 100 years and much of the rise may be related to the increase in global mean temperature....

Average sea level is expected to rise as a result of thermal expansion of the oceans and melting of glaciers and ice-sheets. For the IS92a scenario [IS = IPCC Scenario], assuming the 'best estimate' values of climate sensitivity and of ice melt sensitivity to warming, and including the effects of future changes in aerosol concentrations, models project an increase in sea level of about 50 cm from the present to 2100. This estimate is approximately 25% lower than the 'best estimate' in 1990 due to the lower temperature projection, but also reflecting improvements in the climate and ice melt models. Combining the lowest emission scenario (IS92C) with the 'low' climate and ice melt sensitivities and including aerosol effects gives a projected sea level rise of about 15 cm from the present to 2100. The corresponding projection for the highest emission scenario (IS92E) combined with 'high' climate and ice-melt sensitivities gives a sea level rise of about 95 cm from the present to 2100. Sea level would continue to rise at a similar rate in future centuries beyond 2100, even if concentrations of greenhouse gases were stabilised by that time, and would continue to do so even beyond the time of stabilisation of global mean temperature. Regional sea level changes may differ from the global mean value owing to land movement and ocean current changes....

Climate change clearly will increase the vulnerability of some coastal populations to flooding and erosional land loss. Estimates put about 46 million people per year currently at risk of flooding due to storm surges. In the absence of adaption measures, and not taking into account anticipated population growth, 50-cm sea-level rise would increase this number to about 92 million; a 1-meter sea-level rise would raise it to about 118 million. Studies using a 1-meter projection show a particular risk for small islands and deltas. This increase is at the top range of IPCC [Intergovernmental Panel on Climate Change] Working Group I estimates for 2100; it should be

Grave digger after the cyclone. Banskhali, Bangladesh.

noted, however, that sea level is actually projected to continue to rise in future centuries beyond 2100. Estimated land losses range from 0.05% in Uruguay, 1.0% for Egypt, 6% for the Netherlands, and 17.5% for Bangladesh.

IPCC Second Assessment Synthesis of Scientific-Technical Information Relevant to Interpreting Article 2 of the UN Framework Convention on Climate Change, Geneva, 1995, pp. 5–6, 9–10.

The 1987 Flood

Bangladesh's worst floods for 40 years killed more than 1600 people, left 20 million homeless and destroyed 3.4 million tonnes of crops worth US$1.16 billion. At least 50,000 houses were buried in silt as the floods receded and more than 1100 people died of dysentery and diarrhoea caused by contaminated water. The government announced a US$65 million replanting programme to produce about 1.2 million tonnes of grain. Relief aid worth US$ 100 million was donated by overseas governments.

United Nations Environment Programme, Environmental Events Record, in UNEP News, Geneva, February 1988, Supplement 2.

The 1987-flood distinguishes itself by the fact that all the different types of floods we had in the past happened this time in one and the same season. We had, for example, the usual river-borne monsoon flood brought about by gradual rise of the river-stages. In contrast to this, we also had flash-floods, the quick-rising flood (up to about 4 m in a day in some cases) in Matamuhuri, Monu, Khowai, Bhogai-Kangsa, and in Tangan. Flooding due to tidal effect was also known to occur in 1987. Spring tide in late August, accompanied by depression in the Bay, submerged extensive areas in the coastal areas. The influence of tides in the form of back-water effects inland also held back water from flowing down quickly and as a result more areas were flooded and flood-duration became longer. Back water effects of the principal rivers on the tributaries is another distinctive feature of the 1987-flood.

M. Maniruzzaman Miah, Flood in Bangladesh. A Hydromorphological Study of the 1987 Flood, Academic Publishers, Dhaka, 1988, p. 87.

The 1876 Cyclone

'There was a severe cyclone in the Bay of Bengal on the night of the 31st October 1876. But it was not the wind which proved so destructive, though

Transshipment of goods as high water approaches on the Yangtze. Wuhu, China.

that was terrible enough. It was the storm-wave, sweeping along to a height from 10 to 20 feet, according to different localities; in some places, where it met with any resistance, mounting even higher than that. In the evening the weather was somewhat windy and hazy, and had been unusually hot, the people retired to rest apprehending nothing. Before 11 o'clock the wind suddenly freshened, and about midnight there arose a cry of "the water is on us", a great wave several feet high burst over the country. It was followed by another wave, and again by a third all these waves rushing rapidly onwards, the air and wind being chilly cold. The people were thus caught up before they had time even to climb on to their roof, and were lifted to the surface of the surging flood, together with the beams and thatches of their cottages. But the homesteads are surrounded by palm trees, bamboos and a large thorny species. The people were then borne by the water on the tops and branches of these trees. Those who were thus stopped were saved, those who were not, must have been swept away and were lost. The bodies of the lost were carried to considerable distances, where they could not be identified. The corpses began to putrefy before the water cleared off the ground, so they were left unburied in numbers all over the country. Weather-tossed seamen in the Bay of Bengal saw many corpses floated out from land with the waves. Corpses were flung on to the sea-shore at Chittagong, and living persons were borne hither across an arm of the sea, clinging to the roofs or beams of their own houses, as if upon rafts.'

LIEUTENANT GOVERNOR, SIR RICHARD TEMPLE

'Chittagong District Gazetteer', Chittagong [n.d.], in *East Pakistan District Gazetteer*, Government of East Pakistan, 1970, pp. 45–46.

The 1991 Cyclone

The cyclonic storm of late April was detected as a low pressure area over the southeast bay and the adjoining Andaman Sea on 23 April 1991. In the satellite pictures taken at SPARRSO from NOAA-II and GMS-4 satellites, the low pressure area remained stationary for two days and gradually concentrated into a depression on 25 April 1991. The depression moved in a west/northwesterly direction, then rapidly intensified into a cyclonic storm at midnight on 26 April and curved towards the north. From 28 April it moved in a northeasterly direction and crossed the Bangladesh coast north of Chittagong port during the night of 29 April and in the early morning hours of 30 April 1991.

Monsoon shower. Dhaka, Bangladesh.

Cyclonic winds started battering the coastal islands of Nijhum Deep, Monpura, Bhola, Sandwip from the evening of that day. The maximum wind speed observed at Sandwip was 225 km/hr. The actual wind speed may have been higher but could not be recorded as the wind measuring device was blown away after this speed was recorded.

Salehuddin Ahmed and Neena Afreen, 'Early Warning and Preparedness', in Hameeda Hossain, Cole P. Dodge, F. H. Abed (eds), *From Crisis to Development. Coping with Disasters in Bangladesh,* The University Press Limited, Dhaka, 1992, pp. 82–83.

In the districts of Chittagong, Cox's Bazar, Noakhali, Laximpur, Feni, Bandarban, Rangamati and Khagrachari, out of a total population of 13 million, it is estimated that 1.17 million were the worst affected, 1.72 million were badly affected and 1.67 million were partially affected.

Based on field reports, loss of human life in this zone was estimated at 131,539. A total of 75,528 dead bodies were reported to have been buried by teams of volunteers, many others may have been swept to the sea. Nearly half a million people were injured due to the cyclone, 864,161 houses were completely damaged and 773,897 houses sustained partial damage. Crops of 130,000 acres of land were totally damaged and 390,000 acres were partly damaged.... Huge losses were caused to salt beds, the shrimp culture, and fishing industries. Nearly 7,000 educational institutions and 3,000 mosques were damaged. Industries suffered the worst blow and the estimated loss in this sector alone was estimated at US$380 million. Total losses were estimated at US$2.07 billion for all sectors.

M. Mokammel Haque, 'Relief in Full Swing', in Hameeda Hossain, Cole P. Dodge, F. H. Abed (eds), *From Crisis to Development. Coping with Disasters in Bangladesh,* The University Press Limited, Dhaka, 1992, p. 33.

A *pallar* in difficulties on the Rupsa. Khulna, Bangladesh.

Following pages: Flooding in the Haor basin in the Maulvibazar and Sylhet Districts, Bangladesh.

Rivers under water
Bangladesh is marshy. The waters flowing into the country with the Ganges in the west, the Brahmaputra in the north and the Surma in the east drain a basin extending over 1.5 million square kilometres, covering five countries and both sides of the Himalayas. Bangladesh is like a funnel through which the bodies of water push towards the sea.

Heavy local rainfall and peak tides reaching land at the same time in two or all three rivers cause disasters affecting up to 40 per cent of the country – much more than the normal annual flooding.

In the worst flood this century, which occurred in 1988, 53 out of 64 districts were partially or completely under water.

Cyclone survivor. Banskhali, Bangladesh.

Above and right: Evacuees. Bhangura, Pabna District, Bangladesh.

Hardship after the disaster

Floods, tornadoes, cyclones and soil erosion are recurring events; the Bangladeshis have learnt to live with them and have developed strategies for coping with them. More than 60 per cent of the population is affected by a regular natural disaster at least once a year.

The real problems, however, often begin after people have survived the disaster. For families on a low income, which applies to most of the population, it is difficult to recover from the loss of boat and home, tools, stored crops and domestic animals and to weather a period without any income. Private money lenders profit from the emergency.

The families of women who have been widowed or cast out also suffer sex discrimination when emergency rations and donated clothes are distributed.

Above: Looking for drinking water.
Bhangura, Pabna District, Bangladesh.

Living with the floods

None of the 65,000 villages in the Ganges and Brahmaputra delta is more than two kilometres from a navigable waterway. That means that the floods come upon them quickly, especially when dams on the other side of Bangladesh's land borders are opened without warning.

People stay in their flooded homes for as long as they can, lifting their fireclay ovens first on to the bed and then on to a raft of banana-tree trunks.

Snakes, like the people, flee to the roofs; if there are too many deaths from snake-bites, people seek refuge on the dams but are often driven away by the authorities. Or they find room in reception centres and wait for the water to subside.

In the meantime gangs in boats – fitted with engines from water pumps – loot the abandoned houses. Farmers set up fish pots near the collapsed dams and have an easy haul of fish trapped in the flooded rice fields.

Left: The Mollik brothers, Sonaullah and Azizul, have no land and, during the flooding, no work either, because the landowner's fields in which they work as day labourers are under water after a dam has been breached.
Kazipur, Sirajganj District, Bangladesh.

After the 1991 cyclone. A helicopter brings emergency rations for survivors on Sandwip island, Chattagram District, Bangladesh.

Act of God

On average 80 tropical cyclones, typhoons or hurricanes, as they are called depending on which part of the world they occur in, build up over the seas between latitudes 30 degrees south and 30 degrees north every year. Bangladesh, which has the Himalayas behind it and is open to the flat funnel-shaped coast on the Gulf of Bengal, is an ideal target for the devastating whirlwinds from mid-April to the end of May and from early October to mid-December – before and after the monsoon season.

One of the earliest recorded cyclones destroyed the area of what is now Barisal in 1584. In October 1876 a cyclone claimed 200,000 lives in a 20-metre-high storm flood in Barisal, Noakhali and Chittagong – an enormous number, given the population at the time.

In 1970 an estimated half a million people died in what was the worst cyclone until 1991, when the victims numbered 140,000.

With better satellite monitoring, the warning time has now been increased by valuable hours and several hundred cyclone-protection buildings have been erected on concrete piles up to 13 metres tall.

Remembering the disaster on the night of 29 to 30 April 1991, 800,000 people left the endangered coastal belt and islands after a storm warning in 1994. The cyclone came in the late afternoon and the ebb tide broke the incoming storm tide. On this occasion, rather more than 200 people died, although the cyclone was similar in strength to that of three years earlier.

Left: In Patenga harbour, Chittagong, Bangladesh.

The maximum wind speed in the 1991 cyclone was 225 kilometres an hour – measured on Sandwip island before the measuring instrument was blown away. It was spotted on 23 April as a depression moving north-northwest, two days later becoming a cyclone that gradually turned northeast, with the diameter of its cloud vortex growing to 600 kilometres.

The eye of the cyclone touched Chittagong and Patenga, Bangladesh's main port, where cargo ships, floating docks and fishing boats were flung ashore.

Above: Banskhali, Chattagram District, Bangladesh.

Only coconut palms and betel-nut trees were strong enough to stand up to the wind; they saved many people's lives on the night of the flood and when the water receded they acted as a screen, holding the dead bodies back.

Of those who were washed out to sea or killed away from home in their boats, only those registered in the last census or with fishermen's unions could be declared victims. The official figure did not include the unregistered, who lived on the shoals that appear at certain seasons, or the migrant workers employed in the prawn farms on the moonlit night of the cyclone.

Staring death in the face. Banskhali, Chattagram District, Bangladesh.

Bitter rice

The way to the distribution point for emergency rice rations lies across the dykes in which rotting bodies drifting in the rice fields are buried for lack of any other land.

It was not until several weeks later that the salt water lying over the growing or ripe rice after the 1991 cyclone was finally washed away by the monsoon rain. By then the stalks and seeds had already rotted. Cut rice ready for threshing had been washed out to sea, together with the new seeds and seedlings.

Famine would threaten the following year. This was due to the money policy dictated by the aid business as well as to the failure of the harvest. The devaluation of the national currency and the abolition of price fixing led to an increase in rice prices. Many of the cyclone victims were unable to buy basic food because a large amount of the money donated for them had been diverted.

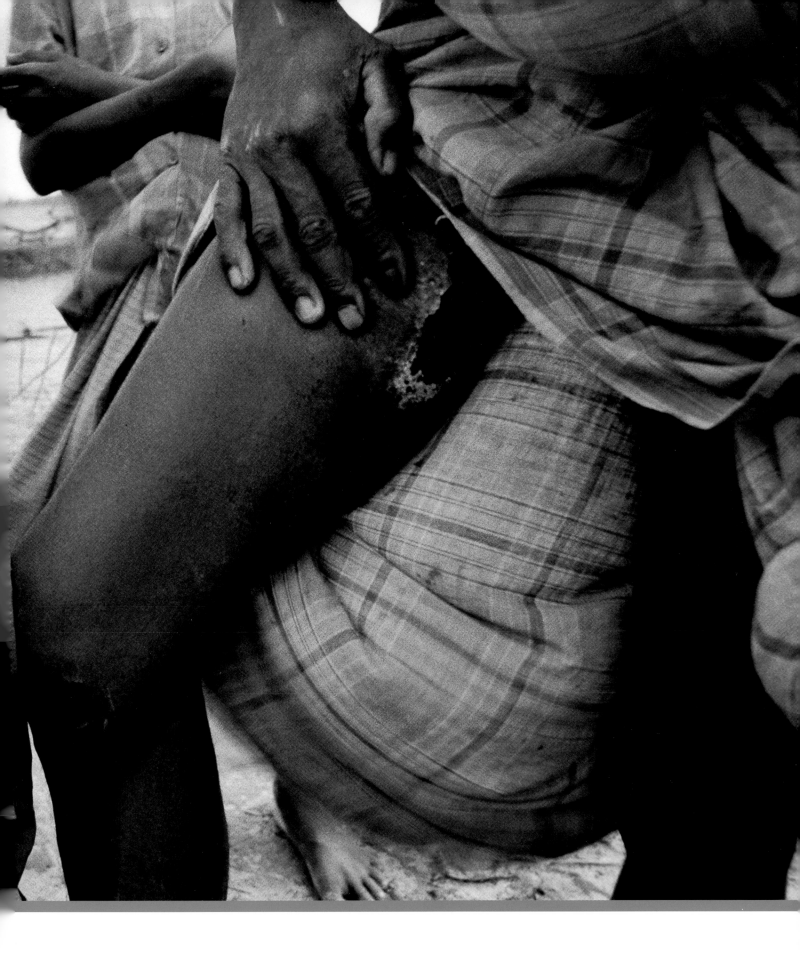

Banskhali, Chattagram District, Bangladesh.

'How big is a woman's heart? Why shouldn't she die?'
So spoke a male cyclone survivor.

Between a third and half of the population were killed by the 1991 cyclone and storm flood in the directly affected areas on the unprotected islands in the curve of the delta and along the coastal belt between Sitakunda and Chakaria.

In many places over four-fifths of the dead were women and children. The life in *purdah* decreed by tradition and religious law meant that women had to stay behind – if their husbands were away working – until it was too late.

On the night of the flood the five-metre-long sari became a death trap. Women who survived hid in the brackish water of ponds until passers-by brought clothes. And if they took them from dead bodies themselves, they were traumatized by the feeling of guilt at still being alive.

Below and right: Victims of epidemic in an emergency hospital on the island of Kutubdia. Cox's Bazar District, Bangladesh.

The aftermath

After the cyclone, the pondwater in the affected areas which is used for all domestic purposes, bathing and drinking, was polluted by dead bodies and rotting animal carcasses, fallen trees and decaying vegetation. Nevertheless, people continued to drink the water. Diarrhoea epidemics and cases of cholera broke out.

In many places the nearest pump wells were too far away for exhausted people who had been without food for several days. Salt water had penetrated most of the wells and had to be pumped out before water-purification tablets could begin to work.

On remote islands many survivors were still dependent on emergency drinking-water rations dropped by helicopters two weeks after the disaster. Or they had to collect rainwater.

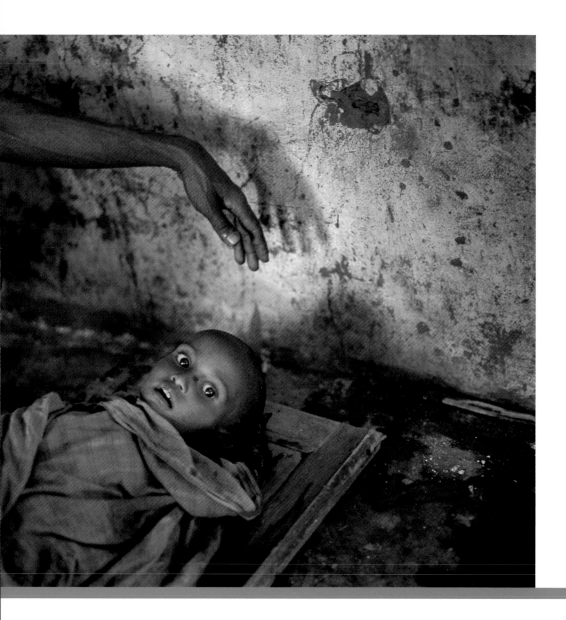

On the edge of Char Balaki in the Meghna. Bandar Gazaria, Munshiganj District, Bangladesh.

Erosion of living space
The swollen river sweeps away the land of 2,500 people. Every evening families move closer together, fearful of being carried away in the night. With luck the island will survive the rainy season. They share a common fate and cannot move away. Already there is not enough money for the boatman who takes the children to school.

The living space of millions of people settled by the rivers and on the chars (the alluvial islands on the rivers) is continually under threat from the silent or insidious disaster.

An island disappears into the sea

Abul Kalem is 55 years old and in poor health. He used to be a farmer. Eight years ago he lost his land through coastal erosion; he had nothing left that he could sell to pay for a move to the mainland. Since then he has built his home in four different places; for the past year he has been living on the dyke, on the outer edge of the island. With his daughter and three sons aged between seven and seventeen, he lives by recycling goods left behind by the people who move away. They break up bricks from collapsed buildings and sell the ballast to a contractor reinforcing the only road on the island, which is becoming shorter and shorter.

Sandwip is emerging and disappearing at the same time. No part of the island is more than a hundred years old. From the northwest the waters of the great river Meghna are breaking in. From the southwest the sea currents are undermining the base of the island and causing the embankments to collapse.

The remains of its main town, once in the middle of the island, are now on the edge. A chronicle of natural destruction: in 1993 the court building, the post office and the district authority guesthouse; in 1994 the telegraph office, the Bangladesh Water Development Board guesthouse, the bank, the hospital and the main street. While the mosque is being gradually washed away, the residents are building a new settlement closer to the centre of the island.

Above, top right and bottom right: Sandwip island, Chattagram District, Bangladesh.

Top left: Evacuated houses on Char Balaki in the Meghna. Bandar Gazaria, Munshiganj District, Bangladesh.

Middle left, bottom left and above: Moving on the Padma. Lohajong, Munshiganj District, Bangladesh.

Ecological refugees

The only option left to the *nadishikosti* (people uprooted by the river), who have repeatedly lost their living space through erosion and have no contacts in the towns, is to migrate to thinly populated outlying areas and new chars.

The new arrivals easily fall victim to landowners, *jotedars*, who control newly emerged land with the help of intimidation gangs and exploit the landless under the guise of bogus cooperatives.

The soil in Bangladesh is so extraordinarily fertile that a family can earn a livelihood from farming even the smallest plot. That is why an average of 800 people per square kilometre crowd so closely together despite the constant threat to life from the uncontrollable forces of nature.

In 1960 every Bengali was a landowner. Now a third are landless and 35 per cent of all legal cases relate to land disputes.

Land on water

Apart from a few hilly areas, Bangladesh is an alluvial plain. The gradient of the Meghna, in which water from the Ganges-Padma and the Brahmaputra-Jamuna flows to the sea, drops from 12.5 centimetres in the north to less than 2.5 centimetres per mile towards the coast.

As it slows down, the river can no longer carry silt. The silt is first deposited on the flooded fields, then along the embankments; finally it forms islands in the river which can sometimes disappear again within a year.

The inhabitants of charland often build their houses on stilts before the new land emerges from the water. It then slowly rises to beneath the floors of the houses, only to be washed away again.

Above and opposite: River dwellers. Sibchar, Madaripur District, Bangladesh.

Left: Charland fishermen on the Jamuna in flood. Bhuapur, Tangail District, Bangladesh.

Below: Jute being carried on the Jamuna. Bhuapur, Tangail District, Bangladesh.

River migration

Repeated flood disasters and tectonic activity moved the Brahmaputra westwards into an old overflow between 1787 and 1830.

The river, up to 16 kilometres wide, continues to deviate even after it has become the Jamuna and flows in a different bed. Its morphology changes constantly and in the rainy season it brings the floods needed to make the farmland fertile.

2
Management of Nature

Who Owns Running Water?

Running water in a natural stream is not the subject of property, but is a wandering, changing thing without an owner, like the very fish swimming in it, or like wild animals, the air in the atmosphere, and the negative community in general.

Samuel C. Wiel, 'Running Water', in *Harvard Law Review*, vol. XXII, no. 3, Cambridge, Mass., 1909, p. 213.

Bangladesh and India's Politics of Water

Any water potential is only as good as its use. East Bengal was always an irrigation-poor part of undivided India and of Pakistan when it was a wing of that country. Floods and drainage were regarded as its principal problems, which they are – for half the year. During dry months, however, irrigation is obviously necessary as much as supplementary irrigation during the monsoon. The very destructive floods of 1954, 1955 and 1956 first turned attention towards water conservation.

B.G. Verghese, *Waters of Hope. Integrated Water Resource Development and Regional Cooperation within the Himalayan-Ganga-Brahmaputra-Barak Basin*, Academic Publishers, Dhaka, 1990, p. 79.

A water-sharing agreement was made between Bangladesh and India in 1985 but the Government of Bangladesh claims its neighbour will not convert what was a memorandum of understanding into a permanent arrangement. A current cause of controversy is the Farakka Barrage which India built on the Ganges just outside the borders of Bangladesh. This was designed to regulate the amount of water in the Hoogly river, which flows out of the Ganges and south through West Bengal to Calcutta. However, data shows that the amount of water going down the Hoogly in regular flood has been reduced from 130,000 to 80,000 cusec. (A cusec is the flow of water in cubic feet per second.) The Bangladesh Government claims the extra 50,000 cusec are being diverted into Bangladesh, adding to their problem. The Farakka Barrage can also be used to prevent water going down the Ganges into Bangladesh during the dry season and in April 1989, with the threat of a drought hanging over their country, the Bangladesh Government produced figures showing that only 19,373 cusec instead of the normal 38,750 cusec were flowing down the Ganges into Bangladesh. There is no doubt that by using the Farakka Barrage, India can control the amount

Preceding pages: Preparing a rice field. Mongla, Bagherhat District, Bangladesh.

At the bridge by the Hill Tracts. Ramu, Bangladesh.

of water coming into Bangladesh via the Ganges but the extent to which this is done is open to debate.

Jim Monan, *Bangladesh: The Strength to Succeed*, Oxfam, Oxford, 1989, p. 27.

By the year 2000 Bangladesh will need to increase food production to 25 million tonnes in order to remain self-sufficient. And to achieve this it will have to bring at least 3.75 million hectares under irrigation by that date as against an ultimate potential of 4.45 million hectares. The object of the National Water Plan (1985–2005) is to develop Bangladeshi water resources so as to maximise both agricultural and fisheries production, apart from providing adequate water supplies for domestic and industrial use, navigation, salinity control and environmental management.

B.G. Verghese, *Waters of Hope. Integrated Water Resource Development and Regional Cooperation within the Himalayan-Ganga-Brahmaputra-Barak Basin*, Academic Publishers, Dhaka, 1990, p. 80.

After a recent wave of flooding that killed at least 2,000 people in South Asia, Bangladesh has renewed demands that India and Nepal agree to control the powerful rivers that flow though their countries.

But political issues in all three countries are preventing efforts to find long-term solutions.

Sanjoy Hazarika, 'Powerful Rivers and Politics', *International Herald Tribune*, 3 August 1993, p. 6. © The New York Times – 1993.

Dhaka is especially riled by the fact that during the dry season the Indians divert water to the Bhagirathi-Hooghly through a feeder canal that starts behind the barrage. In so doing, Dhaka asserts, New Delhi is not fulfilling the terms of a water sharing agreement signed by the two countries in 1977.

But the Indian side has its own constraints. A reduction in the water level of the Bhagirathi-Hooghly, which flows past Calcutta, has made it difficult for large ships to reach the Calcutta-Haldia port system. And finally, the problem is one of simple arithmetic: due to increased diversion of water for irrigation much further upstream in India, there just isn't enough water to fully satisfy both sides.

S. Kamaluddin and Jayanta Sarkar, 'Just Not Enough. Delhi, Dhaka try to share the Ganges' limited water', *Far Eastern Economic Review*, Hong Kong, 20 July 1995, p. 29.

Trying to restore Calcutta's pristine position as a great ocean port is to attempt the impossible. The evolution of large, deep draft vessels in the post-Suez era and of containerisation has changed the mode and concept of international shipping. Calcutta has had its day. It has had to yield to Haldia

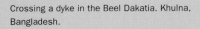
Crossing a dyke in the Beel Dakatia. Khulna, Bangladesh.

which came up 20 years ago as an auxiliary port but has now become the principal port. Haldia too has its problems even though it lies just below the Balari bar, long the troublesome governing bar in navigating the Hooghly to Calcutta, which is to be subjected to a major capital dredging cut. Even with Haldia, Sagar Island, at the mouth of the Hooghly is being used as a lighterage point for vessels seeking to visit Calcutta.

B.G. Verghese, *Waters of Hope. Integrated Water Resource Development and Regional Cooperation within the Himalayan-Ganga-Brahmaputra-Barak Basin*, Academic Publishers, Dhaka, 1990, p. 357.

Cambodia: Rice and War

The country was calm and content, and I wrote after my first visit in 1963 that 'only a war or grotesque mismanagement could produce real hunger or poverty'. This was partly due to the blessings of Nature. Whereas in China, the vagaries of the Yellow and the Yangtze rivers often resulted in flooding or famine, and millions of deaths, the River Tonle Sap, which waters the central rice lands of Cambodia, brings nothing but riches.

Richard West, *War and Peace in Vietnam*, Sinclair-Stevenson, London, 1995, p. 333.

By dramatically increasing rice harvests throughout Cambodia, Pol Pot hoped the country would produce 26.7 million tons of paddy over the lifetime of the plan, recreating what he assumed had been the state-directed plenitude of Angkorean times. Massive irrigation works, it was thought, would make these developments feasible. About half of the production was to be kept aside for seed, food, and 'reserves and welfare'. The exported surplus would earn $1.4 billion in foreign exchange. The income, in turn, was to be used to purchase farm machinery, tools, fertilizer, and insecticide to increase agricultural production. Roughly two-thirds of the income was to be redirected to the zones producing the rice, with the remainder held in reserve for national priorities. Defense expenditures were expected to reach $37 million over four years, with the southwestern and northwestern zones, bordering Thailand, receiving $23 million of that figure.

David P. Chandler, *Brother Number One: A Political Biography of Pol Pot*, WestviewPress, Boulder and Oxford, 1992, pp. 123–24. Copyright © 1992 by WestviewPress. Reprinted by permission of WestviewPress.

The Chinese were ready to continue the free delivery of arms and munitions to their Khmer allies so that the latter could defend themselves against an enemy that had also become China's own—Vietnam. But the arrogant

Water, rice and power. Kompong Speu, Cambodia.

Khmer Rouge could not accept this offer. They intended to pay for everything that China gave them, and the means of exchange was rice.

Marie Alexandrine Martin, *Cambodia: A Shattered Society* (translated/edited by Mark W. McLeod), University of California Press, Berkeley, Los Angeles and London, 1994, p. 187. Copyright © 1994 The Regents of the University of California.

On the technical level, the Khmer Rouge did not adequately take into account the local peasants' empirical knowledge when they laid out rice paddies. Those in charge of townspeople clearing lands came from areas of the country where the terrain and soil conditions were different. Furthermore, they followed orders 'from above'. And yet the Khmer Rouge had model zones laid out with fields of one hectare (100 meters on each side) in order to show visitors the glorious achievements of Democratic Kampuchea; everything had to be aligned and measured off to the last centimeter. In both cases, the cadres scorned the topographical conditions that the former owners had respected. In laying out identical squares, they broke the equilibrium between natural conditions and the peasants' ingenuity. Moreover, they introduced the Chinese method of replanting at the expense of Khmer methods, which were more appropriate for local varieties, and yields fell....

The leaders wanted to build a new Cambodia that would equal the period of Angkor. Yet they could not engage in temple building: aside from the fact that they lacked the technical knowledge, a Marxist regime must avoid religion. It thus had to focus on the economy. So they displayed an irrigation network exceeding the grandeur of those Angkor's monarchs carried out.

Marie Alexandrine Martin, *Cambodia: A Shattered Society* (translated/edited by Mark W. McLeod), University of California Press, Berkeley, Los Angeles and London, 1994, pp. 177–78. Copyright © 1994 The Regents of the University of California.

A 1980 examination of the Angkor era water-management system demonstrates that Yaśovarman's lake was not a critical source of water for the Angkor region's agricultural production in a technical sense, though as the focus of Khmer religion, it was important symbolically in the Khmer system of 'theocratic hydraulics'. Archaeologists have assumed that water seeped through the dyke base of Yaśovarman's lake (which measured 6.5 kilometres long by 1.5 kilometres wide) into collector channels outside the dyke, which subsequently carried the water to surrounding fields. But studies conducted in the late 1970s found that Angkor-era agriculture was based instead on bunded-field transplanted wet-rice cultivation that allowed the planting of approximately fifty million fields. In the Angkor region floodwaters would

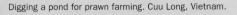

Digging a pond for prawn farming. Cuu Long, Vietnam.

slowly rise from the Great Lake, the Tonle Sap, to its tributaries, but would rapidly recede after the rainy season. A network of dams and bunds diverted and retained the receding floodwaters of the Great Lake after the rainy season. The Khmer lacked the technology to build large-scale dams that could have allowed an integrated region-wide hydraulic system; instead they depended on a network of small, simple earthworks on minor streams to retard and spread floodwaters into clay-based ponds, which stored the water for later use. Archaeological evidence demonstrates that Angkor itself was not a major centre of this water-management network but rather the hill Phnom Kulen, which was located upriver from Yaśovarman's lake some fifty kilometres northwest of Angkor. Phnom Kulen was near the headwaters of the Siemreap (river), which flowed from that area through Angkor to the Tonle Sap. A network of small earth dams regulated the flow of water downstream from Phnom Kulen to Angkor.

Kenneth R. Hall, 'The Temple-based Political-Economy of Angkor Cambodia', in Nicholas Tarling (ed.), *The Cambridge History of Southeast Asia*, vol. I, *From Early Times to c. 1800*, Cambridge University Press, Cambridge, 1992, pp. 230–31.

Burma: Rice under Rulers

The isolation from the coast of the Burmese core region in the north, except for a brief period during the reigns of Bayinnaung (1551–81) and his son Nandabayin (1581–99) when the capital was at Pegu, sharply contrasted with the Chakri dynasty's integration of its rice economy with external trade. The main disincentives to the early expansion of the rice economy in the delta would appear to have been the prohibition of rice exports and the diversion of supplies, collected as tax, to the northern dry zone where the escalation of war under the early Konbaung rulers effected a heavy depletion of manpower and food supplies. The lack of economic incentive, combined with the hazards of malaria in newly opened areas, limited rice acreage to clusters of settlements.... By the last decades preceding the British conquest in 1852, the economic disparity between coast and interior was less significant. There was considerable economic growth in the delta which emerged as the chief granary of the Konbaung dynasty.

J. Kathirithamby-Wells, 'Forces of Integration: Religion, Charisma and Resource Control', in Nicholas Tarling (ed.), *The Cambridge History of Southeast Asia*, vol. I, *From Early Times to c. 1800*, Cambridge University Press, Cambridge, 1992, p. 579.

Harvesting floating rice in the Western Baray (reservoir). Angkor, Cambodia.

The balance of trade of colonial Burma did not experience a single year of deficit from 1886 to 1940. Even the Depression years did not produce trade imbalances, attesting to the relative strength of the foreign sector of the colonial economy to withstand deteriorating world market conditions. In fact, there were some signs of slump in rice exports in the the late 1920s under the competing pressure of other exporting Southeast Asian countries. Yet the continual trade surplus of rice and other export products throughout that period reflected the natural strength and relative richness of the Burmese economy.

Mya Maung, *The Burma Road to Poverty*, Praeger, New York, 1991, p. 58. Copyright © 1991 by Mya Maung. Reproduced with permission of Greenwood Publishing Group, Inc., Westport, CT.

[The case of Maung Pyone – a farmer of the Delta Region.] Maung Pyone has tilled the soil since childhood, planting, reaping, and harvesting of paddy with his parents in his village. He inherited fifteen acres of land (less than the upper limit of twenty acres set by the government for eligibility to receive agricultural loans) from his father and earned his livelihood. Prior to 1962, during the civilian government era, he could sell his paddy in the field (standing rice crop) to the state buyer who visited his village and entered into a contract with him for rice for the state buying depot located in a town some five miles away from his village. He had an option to sell to buyers other than the state buying depots and received an agricultural loan from the village State Agricultural Bank at 6 percent. The repayment of the loan could be made in kind and so he would deal with the state buyer of his rice after he milled the paddy with a private rice mill. Occasionally, he would sell in the private market depending on the price differential between its price and the price offered by the state.

In 1962, everything changed when the government [Revolutionary Council] nationalized private mills and the entire private rice market. His option of private sale was virtually wiped out. He had to enter into a contract with the new team of Corporation No. 1, formerly S.A.M.B. [State Agricultural Marketing Board], under the new system. It seemed attractive at first in terms of receiving lower interest rate loans (3 percent instead of 6 percent repayable in kind) from a new People's Bank and cash from advance sale at a higher price (the maximum of K3.85 per basket) than the maximum price of K3 per basket offered by the former S.A.M.B.'s buying depots of the civilian government....

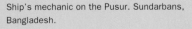

Ship's mechanic on the Pusur. Sundarbans, Bangladesh.

63

However, Maung Pyone, learned very early on that this so-called interest-free loan in the form of the advance sale received was substantially less beneficial to him than the higher prices he could have obtained if he had had the option to sell his paddy to private buyers at a later date.

It seemed that the hedging against the risk of a downward slide in price provided by this forced future contract benefited the government, which had a monopoly of internal and external trade, more than Maung Pyone, since the latter had to give up the opportunity of a higher return with no option in case of upward movements of price. This opportunity cost to the farmers underlined the spontaneous development of an unofficial market. In fact, the education he received was that the inefficient rationing system introduced by the government in towns across Burma had created a buoyant market in which the price of rice was several times higher than the price at government shops....

He found ways to evade the forced sale under the new system by mixing the paddy he had to deliver with sand, pebbles, and other condiments, or selling his *wunsah* paddy to ready buyers, or bribing corrupt officials. An interesting story of how a farmer like Maung Pyone tricked the government buyer relates to selling his paddy at the right time of the day during the harvesting season when the contracts of advanced purchase are due. For instance, the harvesting occurs in rural Burma during the winter months and the harvested paddy weighs heavier when wet with dew at night or in the early morning hours....

Maung Pyone also learned from the only newspaper, *Working People's Daily*, that in Rangoon and elsewhere many persons, including high military commanders, were occasionally purged, arrested, and jailed for engaging in activities considered as 'Opposition to the Construction of the Socialist Economy'. He became skillful and educated in how to avoid being caught as well as developing connections with Party members, powerful officials, and private dealers for his economic survival. He also saw, in the river, boats of dealers from urban centers busily lined up along the side of government barges buying rice from the state officials who were in charge of hauling rice to the cities. In addition to rice, other crops and basic necessities began to disappear from the shelves of government shops throughout Burma, and the foundation of a parallel economy infested with black marketeering was firmly established.

Mya Maung, *The Burma Road to Poverty*, Praeger, New York, 1991, pp. 125–28. Copyright © 1991 by Mya Maung. Reproduced with permission of Greenwood Publishing Group, Inc., Westport, CT.

Landing stage on the Saigon river. Vietnam.

Vietnam: Rice and Liberation

'You and your like are trying to make a war with the help of people who just aren't interested.'

'They don't want Communism.'

'They want enough rice,' I said. 'They don't want to be shot at. They want one day to be much the same as another. They don't want our white skins around telling them what they want.'

'If Indo-China goes...'

'I know that record. Siam goes....'

Graham Greene, *The Quiet American*, Heinemann and The Bodley Head, London, 1973, pp. 99–100.

Ready to move at any instant, we kept our personal encumbrances to a minimum. Two pairs of black pajamas, a couple of pairs of underpants, a mosquito net, and a few square yards of light nylon (handy as a raincoat or roof) were all that a guerrilla owned. The fighters, of course, carried weapons and ammunition in addition, as well as 'elephant intestines,' our term for the long tubes of rolled cotton that could be filled with rice and slung across the back.

In addition to rice, each man's personal larder was rounded out by a small hunk of salt, a piece of monosodium glutamate, and perhaps a little dried fish or meat. The rice ration for both leaders and fighters was twenty kilos a month. Eaten twice a day, at about nine in the morning and four in the afternoon, the ration did not go far. But by and large it was our entire diet, a nutrition intake that left us all in a state of semistarvation.

Truong Nhu Tang, *Journal of a Vietcong*, Jonathan Cape, London, 1986 [*A Vietcong Memoir*, Harcourt Brace Jovanovich, San Diego], p. 158. Copyright © 1985 by Truong Nhu Tang, David Chanoff, and Doan Van Toai.

In 1975, following years of deliberate crop destruction by US and South Vietnamese troops as part of a Resource Denial Program, rice production dropped to an average of 162 kg per capita, nearly half the required nutritional amount.

Elizabeth Kemf, *The Month of Pure Light: The Regreening of Vietnam*, The Women's Press, London, 1990, p. 120.

The move to collectivize the agricultural sector in the South also began in early 1978 and accelerated during succeeding months. A decision to move expeditiously toward the adoption of large-scale collectivization throughout the country had already been reached in 1974, prior to the end of the Vietnam War. The program, known as the New Management System, was confirmed at the Fourth Party Congress in December 1976. It represented

Loading rice. Bassein, Burma.

an enormous gamble, because widespread dissatisfaction among private landholding peasants in the South could have a catastrophic effect on grain production. In order to minimize the risk, the regime followed the gradualist approach that it had originally borrowed from China and applied during the earlier collectivization campaign in North Vietnam.

William J. Duiker, *Vietnam: Revolution in Transition*, WestviewPress, Boulder, 1995, p. 147. Copyright © 1995 by WestviewPress. Reprinted by permission of WestviewPress.

The economic aid gap widened. With the American enemy vanquished, the historic animosity between Vietnam and China reasserted itself. The two governments quarreled seriously over Chinese support for the Khmer Rouge regime of Pol Pot in Cambodia, and the Chinese suddenly cut off all of *their* aid in the spring of 1978. The aid gap then widened again. The Vietnamese were drawn into two more wars that further isolated them. At the end of 1978, unable to bear Pol Pot's attacks on their southern border any longer, the Vietnamese invaded Cambodia to overthrow him. China retaliated by launching an invasion of Vietnam's northern frontier. The United States thereupon joined China in organizing an economic boycott of Vietnam. Japan ceased its aid, as did most of the Western European countries. Under American pressure, the international lending institutions—the World Bank, the Asian Development Bank, the International Monetary Fund—denied Vietnam reconstruction loans....

The rice subsidy alone was enormously expensive. One official estimated that it cost three times as much annually as the war in Cambodia. The state stores provided the monthly rice rations at 50 dong a kilogram, which had been the price of rice in North Vietnam in 1956.... Rice on the free market had meanwhile risen to ten times as much, 500 to 600 dong a kilogram. The government had to subsidize the difference but found it more difficult to obtain rice because production in the South fell after collectivization was extended there in 1978. The farmers had little incentive to produce; their share of the harvest had been reduced to about 20 percent. The other 80 percent went to the government in forced rice sales at less than market value—an attempt to hold down the cost of subsidy—and to the 'Red landlords,' as the salaried bureaucrats who ran the cooperatives were derisively called by the peasantry. Natural disasters from typhoons and crop pests, particularly in Central Vietnam and the Red River delta, perennial rice-deficit areas, worsened the problem. The regime had to resort to spending precious hard currency to import rice from India and other Asian countries.

Neil Sheehan, *Two Cities: Saigon and Hanoi*, Jonathan Cape, London, 1992, pp. 14–16.

Incoming tide at the mouth of the Irrawaddy. Burma.

Following pages: Jute. Bhangura, Pabna District, Bangladesh.

The golden fibre

Jute is sown between April and June, before the start of the monsoon, all along the rivers and waterways, where the floods will be at their highest. In July, after the first heavy rain, farmers in the submerged pathways harvest the fibrous plants standing in water up to three metres deep; in September they cut through the roots, still under water. The saturated stalks, two to five metres long, are left in bundles in the water for a few days; with the help of bacteria the two-millimetre-thick fibre begins to separate from the bark. The farmers, standing in the water, finish the peeling process by hand.

After a preliminary rough sorting, the fibres are baled by middlemen at temporary reloading points and then taken to the dealers in *ghasi*, rowing boats, and *pallars*, sailing boats, where they are sorted according to quality. Depending on the quality, they are either exported or processed into sacks for rice, grain and tobacco or carpet backing and camouflage nets – purposes for which synthetic fibres have increasingly been used since 1960. Nonetheless, jute is Bangladesh's biggest export and the country is still the leading producer worldwide.

Morning in the Irrawaddy delta. Burma.

Bamboo being rafted for sale. Teknaf, Cox's Bazar District, Bangladesh.

Lakes in the fields

The network of waterways in Bangladesh extends to nearly 24,000 kilometres.

When the water level in the country rises by six metres in the rainy season and the houses seem to float like islands on their mounds in the flooded fields, an extra area measuring almost 52,000 square kilometres becomes navigable. At that time it is possible to go right into the jute plantations and sugar-cane groves not normally accessible even by clay paths, along *khals* and *dhobas*, canals and narrow ditches, in flat boats and dug-out canoes, *dinghies* and *gachs*.

Harvesting water hyacinths in a bomb crater. Kandal
Province, Cambodia.

The water hyacinth, originating from Latin America, was
popular in Asia as a decorative plant in ponds and
artificial lakes, from which it spread out into the wild
and became a plague. Its floating, fast-growing carpets
block irrigation canals and are a threat to the rice fields.

Left and below: At the end of the tree-felling season in the mangrove swamps. Sundarbans, Bangladesh.

Above: Mangroves being felled near Cape Camau. Nam Can, Minh Hai Province, Vietnam.

Endangered reserve

The Sundarbans are the biggest mangrove belt in the world, covering over 40 per cent of Bangladesh's afforested area. They produce half the annual forestry yield. The name probably comes from the sundari tree, *Heritiera fomes*, of which the forest mainly consists.

The reserve's ecological balance is under threat from the salination of the marshy ground and the narrow winding waterways. The Farakka dam on the Indian side of the border causes the Ganges water flowing into the Sundarbans to silt up and the Gorai, flowing south with a drastically reduced volume, is unable to withstand

the inflow of seawater. As the silt deposits build up, the aerial roots are smothered; this process, together with salination, causes the treetops to die off and the sundari have to be cut down prematurely.

The gewa trees, *Excoecaria agallocha*, are felled in a 20-year cycle. In the middle of *grishul*, the summer or fourth season in the Bangladeshi calendar, the trunks are tied into bundles with chains at the stacking points, pushed into the shipping channels and made fast to rafts to be towed up the Pusur to the paper factory in Khulna. Passing fishing boats collect the wood left behind.

Above: Sundarbans, Bangladesh.

Forestry work in the huge Sundarbans, with not an inch of solid ground and neither roads nor regular shipping links, is dangerous. Mohamed Abdur Razak, a forestry worker from Shyamnagar in Satkhira District, suffered a fractured skull and broken ribs when a chain broke.

300,000 people work in the Sundarbans, gathering resin to treat fishing nets, shell limestone and honey. Every year two to three dozen people in the mangrove forest fall victim to ageing tigers which can no longer catch deer and other hoofed animals.

Above: Woodcutters in the U Minh mangrove forest.
Bach Bien, Minh Hai Province, Vietnam.

After the ecocide

In the second Indochinese war the Americans sprayed the Ca Mau peninsula with more than six million litres of herbicides, destroying half the country's brackish-water mangrove stocks and a quarter of the freshwater mangroves. A programme of reafforestation began in the mid-eighties.

The young mangroves, which in a few years can supply the local population with building wood, roofing thatch, charcoal and tannic acid, are at risk from typhoons and bushfires. The other major threats come from intensive commercial prawn farming and the vast amount of forest clearance it requires.

The war and the Agent Orange containing dioxin which was absorbed into the food chain are meanwhile still claiming victims, including many who were never sprayed themselves – particularly young women, who develop cancer of the uterus and have stillborn or limbless children.

Child suffering from dehydration. Kutubdia,
Cox's Bazar District, Bangladesh.

No 'Wretched of the Earth'

Sustained development should protect the
environment from further destruction and
the world from collapse. Although the
Bangladeshis' contribution to the greenhouse
effect has been minimal, their future is most
at risk from its effects – for instance, the
rising water level. They are already living
in dire poverty. To escape from this is a
fundamental right – whatever restrictions on
growth and consumption the developed world
is calling for.

If the poor were more secure, they would
bring fewer children into the world. If infant
mortality was lower, the poor would not want
so many children.

Every year 300,000 children under the
age of five die of diarrhoea, since the periodic
floods make the land a breeding ground for
diarrhoea epidemics. In the middle of the war
of independence in 1971 an effective way
was found to combat the dehydration and
physical weakness caused by diarrhoea
and cholera. Oral rehydration therapy (ORT)
consists of a pinch of salt and a handful of
sugar, dissolved in clean water.

Every human life is worth saving.

Top and middle: Ramu, Cox's Bazar District, Bangladesh.

Above: Narsingdi District, Bangladesh.

Above: Dhaka, Bangladesh.

Bangladesh's artificial stones

Since the Buddha walked the roads and battlements of Mahasthan, Bangladesh's most ancient city, bricks have become the main building material in a country with virtually no stone. Arranged in a herringbone pattern, they are used to surface connecting paths in the country, mostly on dykes; when broken up, the bricks provide ballast and gravel foundations.

Despite the discovery of onshore natural gas deposits, wood, a raw material which has become scarce, is still used for fuel in most brickworks.

The women and children employed on the manufacture and processing are paid according to the amount of work they do; a day's wages will pay for a kilo of cheap rice.

79

A blind workman heats the rock to help break blocks out of Phnom Chheu quarry. Prey Veng Province, Cambodia.

Cultural barrier

From the 14th century onwards, the countryside between Vietnam's economic metropolis Ho Chi Minh City and Cambodia's capital Phnom Penh belonged to the Khmer empire. In the 17th century it was occupied by the Vietnamese advancing southwards and in 1862 it became part of French Indochina.

Southeast Asia's cultural barrier, separating the Chinese and Indian influences, lies where the Mekong starts to divide into the nine arms of its delta. The face of the landscape also changes at that point, with jungle vegetation and plantations giving way to isolated groups of coconut palms that tower over the rice fields.

Fortifying the coastal embankment. Patenga, Chittagong, Bangladesh.

North-South conflict

The Bangladeshis and the Dutch are both, in very different ways, under threat from the sea. The Bangladeshis continually strive to keep the sea out; the Dutch have turned the sea into some of the world's most fertile land. The Bangladeshis are forced to import food, while the Dutch export it.

Using one kilocalorie of muscular power, a farmer in Bangladesh produces ten kilocalories from the soil per working day, a Dutch farmer ostensibly a great deal more. In fact, however, 15 million Dutch people consume thirteen times as much energy as 115 million Bangladeshis.

Above: Strengthening the earth embankment of a new lock basin. Jugini, Tangail District, Bangladesh.

Right: Digging an irrigation channel. Dithpur, Tangail District, Bangladesh.

Bangladesh and the 'lords of poverty'

The Flood Action Plan will be a once-in-a-century undertaking, a cathedral to Western hydro-technology in Bangladesh. In 1989 the World Bank took over the general management of the project, which will offer the seven leading industrialized nations investment opportunities worth several thousand million dollars.

The plan centres on the control of the Jamuna river, whose massive power of erosion constantly shifts the banks, destroys the ferry landing stages and causes migration of the talweg and the shipping channels of the transport ships sailing from the Indian state of West Bengal up to Assam.

The purpose of the embankments and lock system in the particularly endangered district of Tangail is to provide widespread flood protection and, potentially, a substantial increase in rice production. In the meantime, the change in the water system will be mainly to the advantage of the small section of the population who own land; food supplies for the poor and poorest, who rely heavily on fish as a source of protein, will be severely affected.

However, the Flood Action Plan ignores not only the effects, such as increased unemployment and growing economic decline, but also the existence and future of several million people, for the simple reason that they live between two project areas.

With the Jamuna dammed and flowing faster at a higher level, the chars will be eroded more quickly. Resettling the inhabitants was not even considered, since there is no land on which they can be resettled. Development is turning the people living by the river into exiles and refugees.

Rice fields with bomb craters. Over Prey Veng Province, Cambodia.

The destruction of Cambodia
American B-52s, infringing the kingdom's neutrality, first bombed suspected North Vietnamese installations and sanctuaries on Cambodian sovereign territory early on the morning of 18 March 1969.

This mission, named 'Breakfast', was followed by 'Lunch', 'Snack', 'Dinner', 'Dessert' and 'Supper'. By the time the secret Operation Menu finally came to light in 1973 and Congress put an end to the flights, which had been penetrating further and further into the country, the Americans had dropped a total of half a million tonnes of bombs – more than three times as many as were dropped on Japan at the end of the Second World War. In order to neutralize Communist logistic installations, Cambodia, which was viewed as an extension of the main theatre of war in Vietnam, was if necessary to be bombed back into the Stone Age.

Casualties among the civilian populations were expected, since the surprise effect was part of the strategy and the Cambodian farmers had not taken any precautions; unlike the Vietnamese, they had little experience of bombing and even less reason to anticipate it. Hundreds of thousands of people were probably killed in the free-fire zones, which stretched as far as the outskirts of Phnom Penh.

The craters made by the bombs in the rice fields are now used as fish and prawn ponds.

Left and below: On the road to Tonle Battie temple. Kandal Province, Cambodia.

Rice and war

Rice farmers use traditional methods to try to save the threatened harvest; meanwhile, heavy building machinery is put to work repairing roads used mainly for the benefit of corrupt industries: construction, the timber trade and tourism.

Death is ever-present when working in the fields and along the irrigation canals dried up during decades of war. An estimated 10 million anti-personnel mines are buried in the ground and undergrowth. Because of the continuing armed conflict between government troops and the Khmer Rouge, who deny access to the areas they control, only a few of the unmarked minefields have been cleared since 1992 for agriculture and settlement. It will be generations before the country with the world's highest rate of mutilation from mines is free of them – and more are being laid every day.

In the words of an old Cambodian proverb, rice needs water and war needs rice.

87

Below: Fields being prepared for winter rice. Kandal Province, Cambodia.

The 'first ploughing' ceremony by the king in May marks the start of the rice season and the farming year. Brahmans decide the most auspicious day for the ceremony.

The idea of the ruler ploughing the 'holy furrow' is based on the most ancient epic in Sanskrit literature, the *Ramayana*, dating from the 4th century BC. It relates how King Janaka, ploughing with a golden plough, met a girl he called Sita, the furrow, and how she later became the wife of the god Rama.

After going three times round the holy field, the goddess of vegetation, the lord of the earth and the god of rain are worshipped and the white oxen led to seven silver dishes of rice and other gifts. If they choose grain, the harvest will be good; if they choose grass, the cattle will be stricken by epidemics; if they drink water, enough rain will fall and there will be peace; but if they go to the bowl containing alcohol, there will be fighting in the kingdom.

Above: 'Boro' rice in the seedbed. Sibpur, Narsingdi District, Bangladesh.

'Boro' is the last of the three annual rice harvests in Bangladesh. 'Aus' rice is sown in April and May and harvested from July to August. 'Aman' rice is either sown direct in March or April, or in seedbeds in July, and harvested from November to December.

Rice in the seedbed is lifted from the wet ground in bundles after forty days, covered with damp leaves and taken to be replanted in prepared fields. Either the fields are kept constantly under water or the farmers let the water flow away and dry the ground, flooding it again shortly before the harvest.

In Cambodia and Bangladesh there are varieties of floating rice which grows with the rising tide, up to 15 centimetres in 24 hours. Many Japanese paratroopers jumping from aircraft over Bengal in the Second World War to capture British Burma were drowned because they were not familiar with these varieties, whose stalks reach a height of up to five metres.

Left and above: Funeral procession in the Red River delta. Hai Hung Province, Vietnam.

Above right: Rice farmers resting while replanting on a grave. Mekong delta, Long An Province, Vietnam.

Vietnam's soul in the rice field

Rice is a basic foodstuff and an ingredient in any religious ceremony. Rice is the basis of all life and also has significance in death. Rice is served at weddings and given to coffin makers.

Farmers are buried in the fields they have tilled all their lives, in the belief that their souls will pass into the rice and through it into their descendants.

In a poem Ho Chi Minh, founder of the Indochinese communist party and President of the Democratic Republic of Vietnam (North Vietnam) from 1945 until his death in 1969, compared the tribulations of rice, which acquires its fine white colour through being pounded in the mortar, with the human soul, which becomes stronger through misfortune.

Planting the seedlings in the hottest months is hard work. The women, their arms protected with nylon stockings, move forward along the paths marked with string and plant four seedlings at a time about 20 centimetres apart, taking care to cover the roots with enough mud.

Left: Rice fields before the harvest. Takeo Province, Cambodia.

Above: Harvest and chaff in Phu Xuyen District, Ha Son Binh Province, Vietnam.

Rice country

Rice, *Oryza sativa*, was first grown in the early Holocene period in the southern Yangtze basin in China. From there it spread to the central tropical zones in whose natural marshy and alluvial ground it flourished best.

Funan, the first known civilization in Southeast Asia (1st–6th centuries AD), prospered because the hinterland to its capital near the present Vietnamese–Cambodian border was a naturally humid area suited to rice-growing. With its

resources Funan was able to supply the trade ships which were forced to wait at the tip of the Mekong delta for the wind to change on the voyage from Rome to China.

The development of this marshy, reed- and mangrove-covered area for full-scale rice cultivation was started around 1800 by the Vietnamese Nguyen dynasty. The French continued until 1890, using forced labour, after which mechanized French firms took over. A network of irrigation canals more than 1,300

kilometres long evolved, and this also opened the Mekong delta up to traffic. Vietnam, as part of French Indochina, became the third largest rice exporter.

The Socialist Republic of Vietnam regained this position in the early nineties, after the collectivization introduced in 1975 in the reunification of North and South Vietnam was abolished under the liberalization of the economy and the rice mills were returned to their owners.

Above: Rice harvest. Bassein, Irrawaddy, Burma.

Right: Threshing. Kandal Province, Cambodia.

Rice and society

As a social institution, the rice cycle – preparation, sowing, tending and replanting; watering, harvesting and threshing; burning the straw to ash fertilizer, drying, grinding and selling – occupies virtually the whole of the village population. Everyone is involved, from landowners to gleaners, who make sure that not a single grain is left to waste on the roads where the rice is laid out to dry or at the loading points along the canals.

In the Asian spirit world many gods and beings are connected to rice growing. Farmers ask the local earth spirit for permission before they start to trespass with the plough and they let off fireworks to attract the attention of the rain gods when the monsoon is late. In the barns there are straw effigies of the rice goddess, who is invited to stay until the next sowing and is believed to protect stocks against rats and other pests.

Above: Rice trading. Dhaka, Bangladesh.

The fear of hunger

In most South Asian and Southeast Asian languages the word for rice is the same as the word for eating. 'Have you eaten?' is 'Have you chewed rice?' in Bengali. A meal with not enough rice is not a meal; a handful of rice early in the morning helps the fasters through Ramadan.

Bengal and later Bangladesh have been affected by the worst famines in history. The first, after annexation by the East India Company, claimed an estimated ten million lives or a third of the population between 1769 and 1770. It was not until 1883 that an instrument was created in the Famine Code to control emergency rice supplies in disaster areas.

Three million Bengalis died in 1943 as a result of the war and the passive attitude of the British Government. Furthermore, Britain, which was interested in steel exports, had built more railways in Bengal rather than irrigation canals; and when

famine broke out, the troops had to be supplied first. The Japanese had occupied Burma and thousands of boats were destroyed as a precaution against a Japanese invasion. Rice stocks in the country were blockaded or stockpiled by grain dealers.

Bangladesh's present poverty stems from the 1943 disaster. It was catastrophic for Bengal, which had already had its jute industry deliberately destroyed in the 19th century and subsequently became isolated after the capital of British India was moved from Calcutta to New Delhi in 1912. Memories of the devastating famine led to the introduction, soon after the new nation was created from the former East Pakistan in 1971, of a food distribution system thanks to which the threat of famine in the most serious floods in history in 1987–1988 was averted.

Above: In rice mill no. 6/2. Bassein, Irrawaddy, Burma.

Power and rice

After the Irrawaddy delta was annexed in 1852, the British lifted the ban on rice exports imposed by the Burmese court, which had paralysed rice cultivation. With a new land and tax policy offering incentives for increased production, the delta became the most important rice-growing area in the world.

However, around 1930, when rice was British Burma's main export, the farmers were enormously in debt. Eastern middlemen controlled the whole financial sector. Nevertheless, the 'golden fruit' monoculture continued to expand. In 1942 – when the Japanese took Burma – the Irrawaddy delta produced 3.5 million tonnes a year, half the whole world market.

Impoverishment set in in 1962 with the military coup. The black market virtually became the economy, with farmers seeking to dispose of their harvest after the rice mills had been nationalized, avoiding compulsory sales. Corruption and the economic ignorance of the military soon led to a rice shortage, which was exacerbated by the biggest flood disaster in the history of independent Burma in 1974. In 1988, when the present government suppressed the democratic movement, rice exports had dropped to 20,000 tonnes.

Rice and the end of nature

Rice grows where no other grain would yield such results: in marshy valleys and alluvial deltas, in hot areas and mountain forests. Rice is responsible for Asia's large population, which by 2025 will total nearly five thousand million, as many as the world population in 1968. Over four thousand million will be dependent on rice as a basic foodstuff in Asia; today it is already 2.7 thousand million.

To feed the growing population, 70 per cent more rice has to be produced in the next 30 years. By the year 2000, a super-rice will yield 13 tonnes per hectare per season, one-third more than before. Annual methane emissions into the earth's atmosphere from

the rice-growing areas will increase as a result.

The climatic changes brought about by the greenhouse effect will force agronomists to think more about the salt tolerance of the rice plants. Sea level will probably rise by an estimated 15 to 50 centimetres in the next century, forming river backwaters and deep brackish-water areas in the coastal and delta regions of South and Southeast Asia.

Already there is another problem. This part of the world, which is described as the world's sponge, is suffering increasingly from water shortage through over-use and pollution. More rice has to be grown, but with less and less water.

Above: Delivery and quality control in the rice market. Phnom Penh, Cambodia.

Right: Emergency rations being issued to women farmers. Phnom Penh, Cambodia.

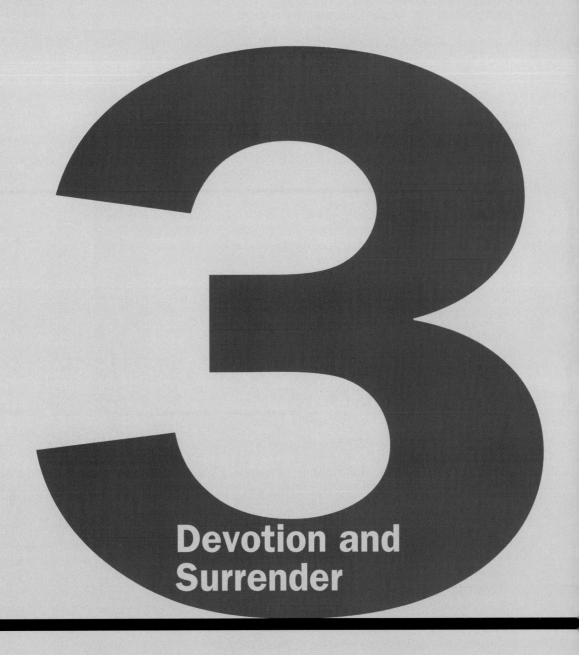

3
Devotion and Surrender

The Emergence of Bangladesh

The people of Lalpukur could not help knowing that a war was brewing across the border; their relatives on the other side never let them forget it. Often they were drummed to bed by the rattle of distant gunfire. But on the whole the fighting was to pass Lalpukur by. And, unlike some of their neighbours, no one in Lalpukur had the energy to join in of their own will. The reason was that the people of Lalpukur were too melancholy. Vomited out of their native soil years ago in another carnage, and dumped hundreds of miles away, they had no anger left. Their only passion was memory; a longing for a land where the green was greener, the rice whiter, the fish bigger than boats; where the rivers' names sang like Megh Malhar on a rainy day – the Meghna, the Dholeshshori, the Kirtinosha, the Shitolokhkha, the majestic Arialkha, wider than the horizon. Rivers which bore the wealth of a continent to their land, from Tibet, from the Himalayas. Rivers overflowing with bounty, as wide as seas, their banks invisible from one another.

Lalpukur could fight no war because it was damned to a hell of longing....

Long before the world had sniffed genocide in Bangladesh, Lalpukur began to swell. It grew and grew. First, it was brothers with burnt backs and balls cut off at the roots. Then it was cousins and cousins of cousins. Then it did not matter; borders dissolved under the weight of millions of people in panic-stricken flight from an army of animals.

Amitav Ghosh, *The Circle of Reason*, Granta/Penguin Books, London, 1994, pp. 59–60. Copyright © 1986 by Amitav Ghosh. Reproduced by permission of Penguin Books Ltd.

True to a tradition that stretches back to before the Buddha, there have been those in Bangladesh who have resisted the presence of the caste-conscious Aryans, the Hindus. At first as outcastes, as dasas and namasudras, the Bangladeshis tended to retreat into the watery swamps of the river deltas, out of reach of the more civilized landlubbers to the west. There they held out as long as possible. At the time of the Buddha they rose up and left Hinduism in large numbers for the certainties of the Buddha's casteless society. For twelve hundred years they were attracted to the Buddha's path and resisted any attempt to force them back into the caste system. When, in the tenth to twelfth centuries, the Sena Dynasty tried to force them into the caste system and to Sanskritize their language, they resisted in the face of great cruelties. They endured this struggle until the emergence of a new casteless society in the form of Islam, under which, for the next half-millennium (1200 to 1757), they lived without fear of Hindu caste rules.

Preceding pages: Durga sinking. Calcutta, West Bengal, India.

Rice offering after a cremation on the Baghmati, a tributary of the Ganges. Kathmandu, Nepal.

When the British wrested control from the Muslims, they initially catered to Bengal's Hindu minority, playing off that minority against the formerly powerful Muslim majority. During the first 120 years, the British destroyed the bases of Muslim society: the madrassahs, the courts based on Persian and Muslim law, the army, and the government system.... Only in the 1890s, when the favored Hindus began challenging British rule, did Britain make the Muslims their new favorites....

Nevertheless, when Bengal was divided in 1905, the Muslims at first heeded their Hindu neighbors' appeal to remain loyal to a unified Bengal and almost joined the anti-British rebellion. But as soon as Hindu forces outside Bengal turned the protest into an All-India and Hindu movement, the Muslims backed out. For they saw that Hindus meant to maintain their superiority not only in Bengal but also in a united, Hindu-dominated India. Yet in that first moment of agitation, when the protest seemed to be about Bengali nationalism and not about Indian or Hindu nationalism, modern Bangladesh was born, at least in spirit....

Though it is anathema to say so in today's Bangladesh, the truth is that the high literary tradition of Bangla was carefully developed in the late nineteenth century mostly by Hindus, who used Bangla to help impart to their province the sense of identity of a modern nation-state in the European style. As for Bengal's Muslims, during this period of Hindu revival they were in the throes of a deep reexamination of their Muslim roots and were writing in Puthi ['Mussalmani Bangla', a language filled with Urdu, Arabic, and Persian]. Not until the first decade of the twentieth century did the Muslims begin turning to Bangla literary style and tradition, and not until the 1960s did they vociferously endorse a wholehearted Bengali ideology. Thus one result of the united Bengal movement of 1905–12 was that Bengali Muslims began the process that would lead to the language movement and the ultimate acceptance by educated Bangladeshis of the high literary tradition of Bangla developed by Hindus in the nineteenth century. Not until this transition occurred did Bangla become the language behind Bangladeshi nationalism and the great modern language it is today....

Having grown to maturity before the initial battle over Bengal partition, he [Rabindranath Tagore] soared to his most creative heights in that era and elevated the campaign from a crass political action to a major intellectual event. His ability to do so sustained the movement even after he broke with its terrorist aspects and helped convince the more reasonable representatives of British rule that Bengal should not be divided....

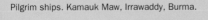

Pilgrim ships. Kamauk Maw, Irrawaddy, Burma.

As for Nazrul, he both represented a much younger generation and held different world views from those of his fellow poets. Like Tagore he was an autodidact, but unlike him he was not a dilettante, although he was profligate in practical affairs and philosophically undisciplined. For Nazrul devoted his life to poetry. He did not have grander aims, such as trying to found a university or to reshape society, except through his poetry and songs....

Rebel was an instant success. Reprinted immediately in larger press runs, it became the mood piece among university students who, forty years later, in 1960, were to lead the Bangladesh independence movement. For Nazrul's poem broke the chains of liberalism and opened up a near nihilistic vision of libertarian violence.

> *Proclaim Hero, Proclaim*
> *Towering high is my head....*
> *I am invincible, insolent and cruel for ever.*
> *I am the dancing demon on the day of the doom,*
> *I am the cyclone; I am destruction.*
> *I am the terrible terror, the curse of the earth.*
> *I am to be stopped by none.*
> *I tear all things to tatters.*
> *I am indiscipline, I am chaos.*
> *I trample down all fetters, all rules and regulations.*
> *I acknowledge no law whatsoever....*
> *I am the Rebel, the rebellious son of the Lord of the universe...*
> *I am the Hero in revolt for ever!*
> *I have risen beyond the universe, alone,*
> *With my head ever held high!...*

(Trans. Mizanur Rahman, 1966)

His [Nazrul's] appeal reached across educational boundaries, for he expressed what was in the people's hearts. That is why his works were so important to the politics of Sheikh Mujib. The revolt against Pakistan had to do with culture: the immediate culture of Bangladesh and the distant culture of the Pakistanis. What Nazrul brought to the fray was a Bangladeshi language and a true son-of-the-soil and Muslim voice to counteract the fact that, after all, Tagore was dead and, besides, he had been a man from Calcutta, West Bengal, and India....

Morning rituals on the Hooghly in Calcutta. West Bengal, India.

By the 1960s in East Bengal, the works of Tagore, Nazrul, and a balladeer named Jasmiuddin, who reached out to villagers, comprised the literary foundations of the liberation movement. Tagore, whose centenary was celebrated in the 1960s, undoubtedly appealed to the best educated, to those of Brahmo sensibilities, and to progressives. Nazrul was favored by students, young rebels, teachers, and the near-educated. Jasmiuddin spoke for the peasants. Meanwhile, in the villages, countless unheralded local bards wrote poems of love, nature, and revolt. Together, all these verses voiced the aspirations, the yearnings, and the beliefs of what was to become a new nation.

James J. Novak, *Bangladesh: Reflections on the Water*, Indiana University Press, Bloomington, 1993, pp. 139–40, 160–61, 163.

Burma: A Regime against its People

Anyone who wishes to have a foretaste of hell should visit the Naf river that forms the boundary between Burma and Bangladesh. Each day groups of traumatised Muslim refugees from Burma's Arakan state paddle their small wooden boats across this mile-wide stretch of water. They say soldiers have confiscated their land, food and crops, occupied mosques, burnt their religious texts and raped the women in a systematic effort to drive them from Burma….

To quote Amnesty International, the whole country is a 'prison without bars'. Torture of prisoners in detention has been routine. One torture known as 'walking the seashore', it said, involved prisoners walking on their knees on sharp gravel. Others were forced to endure 'the helicopter' – hanging by their feet from a ceiling hook or a rotating fan and being beaten with whips and clubs while suspended. After beatings and knife cuts, salt, urine and curry powder were applied to the open wounds.

Jon Swain, 'The Killing Fields: Another Harvest', in *The Sunday Times Magazine*, 28 June 1992, p. 25. © Times Newspapers Limited, 1992.

The Buddhist view of kingship does not invest the ruler with the divine right to govern the realm as he pleases. He is expected to observe the Ten Duties of Kings, the Seven Safeguards against Decline, the Four Assistances to the People, and to be guided by numerous other codes of conduct such as the Twelve Practices of Rulers, the Six Attributes of Leaders, the Eight Virtues of Kings and the Four Ways to Overcome Peril. There is a logic to a tradition

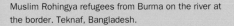

Muslim Rohingya refugees from Burma on the river at the border. Teknaf, Bangladesh.

which includes the king among the five enemies or perils and which subscribes to many sets of moral instructions for the edification of those in positions of authority. The people of Burma have had much experience of despotic rule and possess a great awareness of the unhappy gap that can exist between the theory and practice of government....

The words 'law and order' have so frequently been misused as an excuse for oppression that the very phrase has become suspect in countries which have known authoritarian rule. Some years ago a prominent Burmese author wrote an article on the notion of law and order as expressed by the official term *nyein-wut-pi-pyar*. One by one he analysed the words, which literally mean 'quiet-crouched-crushed-flattened', and concluded that the whole made for an undesirable state of affairs, one which militated against the emergence of an alert, energetic, progressive citizenry. There is no intrinsic virtue to law and order unless 'law' is equated with justice and 'order' with the discipline of a people satisfied that justice has been done. Law as an instrument of state oppression is a familiar feature of totalitarianism. Without a popularly elected legislature and an independent judiciary to ensure due process, the authorities can enforce as 'law' arbitrary decrees that are in fact flagrant negations of all acceptable norms of justice. There can be no security for citizens in a state where new 'laws' can be made and old ones changed to suit the convenience of the powers that be. The iniquity of such practices is traditionally recognized by the precept that existing laws should not be set aside at will. The Buddhist concept of law is based on *dhamma*, righteousness or virtue, not on the power to impose harsh and inflexible rules on a defenceless people. The true measure of the justice of a system is the amount of protection it guarantees to the weakest.

Aung San Suu Kyi, 'In Quest of Democracy', in *Freedom from Fear and other Writings*, edited by Michael Aris, Penguin Books, London, 1991, pp. 170, 176–77. This collection copyright © Aung San Suu Kyi, 1991. Reproduced by permission of Penguin Books Ltd.

There is a clear consensus that Burma cannot return to its former isolation. Political and economic pressures are such that the Burmese now have little option but to accept that they are indeed 'citizens of a wider world'.

And yet the country's future remains uncertain. In the immediate future there will be little challenge to SLORC's authority, and the sheer weight of its military power means that it may well continue to control the country for some years to come. Some Asian commentators have welcomed this in the belief that political stability, however repressive, is a better guarantor

Dragon boat on the Yangtze. Wuhu, China.

of 'human rights' than the upheavals which might follow a change of government. Such arguments carry weight in a region which has seen chronic instability in the course of the twentieth century, and which sees the promise of a new and unprecedented prosperity – provided that political crises do not intervene – in the twenty-first.

However, Burma is exposed to powerful economic and social forces for change. There is a consensus in favour of economic liberalization, but the decisions required to manage reforms demand a degree of technical sophistication that is not readily found in the Burmese (or any other) army. In the past the Burmese government has been able to exercise a high degree of control over the information its citizens receive. This will be increasingly difficult as the country broadens its links with the outside world.

These changes raise the question whether the SLORC regime can adapt. To some extent it is adapting, but not enough. It is still reluctant to take radical but painful measures such as devaluation. In theory the National Convention demonstrates a desire for political evolution, but the army's wish to control proceedings means that its deliberations lack credibility. Burma needs to make far-reaching decisions on such issues as economic reform and the political status of the ethnic minorities. It is very doubtful whether the military elite has the skills – let alone the moral authority – to make those decisions on the Burmese people's behalf. Economic and social changes will reinforce the desire for greater public participation in government.

Burma's past history serves as a reminder that it would be rash to underestimate the durability of a well-entrenched military regime. But the world of the 1990s is much more complex than that of the 1960s. The experience of other socialist and former socialist countries shows how the authority of apparently impregnable regimes may collapse quite suddenly. Sudden crises – such as the death of Ne Win or a series of major public demonstrations – will expose SLORC's vulnerability. Outwardly, Rangoon and other Burmese cities are more relaxed than in the early 1990s, but in practice the regime is as fervently disliked as ever. It will take much more than the present limited economic development to erase the memories of 1988. On the surface, central Burma may be calm, but it retains the potential for major political upheavals.

John Bray, *Burma: The Politics of Constructive Engagement*, Discussion Paper 58, The Royal Institute of International Affairs, London, 1995, pp. 61–62.

On board in the Irrawaddy delta. Burma.

Left and above: The end of the Durga Puja. Calcutta,
West Bengal, India.

The recycling of the goddess

Durga, the 'unfathomable', wife of Shiva, is worshipped
at an annual prayer festival in autumn, the *puja*, as a
symbol of fertility and destroyer of evil.

In the four days of the Durga Puja statues are put
up in tent-like shrines and worshipped and then, on the
last evening, brought to the banks of the Hooghly.
The goddess is also returned and dissolved in a
physical sense. The clay from which her face and
limbs were made goes back into the river from which
it came – and with it the toxic pigments of the paint
with which it has been sprayed. Children living along
the tracks of the adjoining railway seize on the wood
and straw skeletons of the statues as they break up
in the water, to salvage anything usable and saleable
such as silver foil and plastic parts.

Above: Brahmans pouring water from the Hooghly on sacrificial offerings. Calcutta, West Bengal, India.

The cosmic substance

Rivers might alter their course, but their sacred cleansing power remains.

Since the 15th century only a small part of the Ganges has run along its original bed, the Bhagirathi Hooghly, into the sea south of Calcutta. According to the myth it enters the underworld at Sagar island.

At the beginning of the year hundreds of thousands of people flock to Sagar to pray to the river.

A breath of wind from the Ganges or the rivers it feeds is enough to wipe out sins. On the Ganges, Asia's most sacred river, dying promises the end of the cycle of rebirths.

Right: Boatman at *maghreb*, evening prayer. On the river Meghna, Gazaria, Munshiganj District, Bangladesh.

The religion that came by river

When the Ganges, instead of flowing south through the trading centre of Sutanuti, later Calcutta, pushed east and first met the Jamuna, a new frontier opened up.

East Bengal, through which the river began to wind, was largely jungle, and its people, who in contrast to those in West Bengal were not yet aryanized, were animists by religion. They were converted by Muslims arriving by river, who had already had settlements at the mouth of the Meghna since 1200; the farming land they were allocated might have been an incentive. Women were inevitably attracted to Islam, less severe than Hinduism which banished female offspring and practised suttee.

On the way to a wedding. Srinagar, Munshiganj District, Bangladesh.

The land of Bengali

The Namasaduras, the first settlers in the delta on the Bay of Bengal and ancestors of the present Bangladeshis, appeared in Western history in a confrontation with Alexander the Great. They were the troops of the non-Aryan King Nanda, who opposed the Macedonians in 327 BC. Exhausted and cut off from reinforcements, the soldiers begged not to have to fight against the feared strangers, whom Ptolemy called Gangarides. Alexander broke off his campaign and turned westward.

The Bangladeshis are now over 90 per cent Muslim, but they are also heirs to Hindu culture, which spanned a curve from Iran to Afghanistan and the Indus Valley as far as the lower reaches of the Ganges.

Bangladesh was created in 1971 after a period of foreign rule which had begun in 1757 under the East India Company and continued, after Britain partitioned Bengal in 1947, under Urdu-speaking Islamabad (West Pakistan).

East Pakistan's two-week war of liberation, in which there were half a million victims, ended on 16 December 1971. Bangladesh was born, a country where Bengali is spoken – the language in which wandering baul minstrels and boatmen as well as Rabindranath Tagore sing of life on the rivers and in the rain, the unity of man and nature in this country on the water.

Above: Sacrificial gifts on the Ben Ninh Kieu. Cantho, Mekong delta, Vietnam.

Right: Boats at the water festival. Phnom Penh, Cambodia.

The principle of harmony

At New Year, *tet*, fishermen and the houseboat-dwellers who carry goods in the delta bring the river spirits rice and roast chicken on small bamboo rafts, hoping for a good catch and a safe journey.

Towards the end of the rainy season, at the October full moon, the turn of the current in the Tonle Sap as it flows to the sea is celebrated by a water festival. This gave the king of the Khmer, who held the boat processions, the chance to prove to his people that Naga, the mythical water-dweller, had been tamed and the mandate he had been given from heaven was justified.

The awareness of the interconnection between the destinies of heaven, earth and man in the Asian countries regularly hit by environmental disasters has pre-Buddhist and animist roots. Nature is inhabited and man must respect this in everything he does, taking no more from nature than he can give back.

This ecological viewpoint dates back to ancient cosmology. Evaporation corresponds to the chthonic waters of the underworld rising or to the earth's influence on the heavenly order. Rain corresponds to the sunlight shining down, which makes all life possible, or to heaven's influence on earthly things.

Above: Monk and bats at Chu Maha Tup Khmer temple. Soc Trang, Mekong delta, Vietnam.

Right: Members of the Cao Dai clergy outside the temple in Long Hoa. Tay Ninh Province, Vietnam.

Above: Khmer temple at Bac Liêu. Minh Hai Province, Vietnam.

The capture of the Mekong delta in the mid-18th century by the Annamites (Vietnamese) advancing south sparked off a long-standing conflict which until very recently has continued to claim victims in Cambodia and Vietnam.

Hostilities first broke out in 1820 with the Kai revolt, caused by the forced labour of 50,000 Khmers digging the Vinh Te canal between Chau Doc on the Mekong and Ha Tien on the Gulf of Thailand.

After 1975, when the Khmer Rouge brought genocide to Democratic Kampuchea, many members of the harshly persecuted Buddhist clergy, the *sangha*, fled to the Khmer temples in Vietnam, which was otherwise dominated by Confucianism.

Above: Praying in front of the statue of the reclining Buddha
on the terrace of the Shwedagon pagoda. Rangoon, Burma.

Burma is the fifth country – the others being Sri Lanka, Thailand,
Cambodia and Laos – in which Theravada Buddhism is practised.
This only survivor of the hinayanistic schools regards itself as
the original form of the Buddha's teaching, because its text
comes straight from the master's mouth.
    Theravada, unlike Mahayana, Buddhism teaches salvation
through the observance of ethical rules and the eightfold path,
which starts from 'right understanding' and reaches its acme in
'right concentration of the spirit' into the 'four contemplations'.

Members of the military junta escorting pilgrims
to the pagoda festival. Two monks on their way to
a remote shrine. Mawtinsun, Irrawaddy, Burma.

Mawtinsun, formerly Cape Negrais, where the Arakan
mountain range running parallel to the coast of the
Bay of Bengal slopes down to the Andaman Sea, is
a desolate place at the end of the world, a strategic
hinterland, and therefore sheltered by the Rangoon
junta.

Opposite the cape is Diamond Island, with a
lighthouse and a two-storey bungalow from the
British period. The island used to be called Tha
Mee Hla, named after the 'beautiful daughter' of
King Ah Laung Si Thu, who stopped here in year
103 in the Burmese calendar on her way back
from a pilgrimage to Sri Lanka.

Once a year, at the full moon in the month of
Taboung, the pagodas on the sandy hill of the
headland and the smaller pagoda on the last cliff,
flooded at high tide, are visited by thousands of
pilgrims from Bassein, Rangoon, Prome and Upper
Burma.

Left: Monk by the sea. Chaungtha, Irrawaddy, Burma.

Below: Calm as the surface of a still stretch of water. When the crowds of pilgrims have left, U Taik Taki, a hermit from Upper Burma, will stay on for another week at the cape, meditating and fasting. Mawtinsun, Irrawaddy, Burma.

Monks in the resistance

The *sangha*, the order of monks, was infiltrated by the military after the Burmese democracy movement was suppressed in 1988.

In the eastern border areas outside Rangoon's control on the river Salween, militant monks sided with ethnic minorities which had been fighting for independence for decades and with members of the opposition who had fled. This united resistance was always clashing with the Burmese Army, now numbering 300,000 men, and collapsed at the beginning of 1995 under the junta's tactical policy of 'divide and rule'.

Return to Cambodia

The Paris Peace Agreement in October 1991 was intended to resolve the Cambodian conflict, which had started when the Khmer Rouge seized power. The withdrawal of the Vietnamese troops in 1988 was a precondition for settlement of the conflict, which had degenerated into mine warfare.

All four parties in the civil war signed, but the Khmer Rouge later boycotted the implementation by the United Nations Transitional Authority in Cambodia (UNTAC) of the four main points.

A key point in the agreement was the repatriation, 'safely and with dignity', of the 350,000 refugees living in Thai camps since the seventies. And they were promised that they would be able to live safely and with dignity in their old homeland, free from oppression. But the civil war factions could not be completely disarmed, and when darkness fell many of the repatriates buried their new identification cards for the free and fair elections that had been announced for fear of visits by intimidation squads.

By the time the last train arrived in April 1993 in Phnom Penh, from where the repatriates were taken to their chosen destination in lorries or ships on the Mekong, some of the homecomers were already internal refugees again. The mine warfare had never stopped and not enough safe land could be found for settlement and farming. Those of the repatriates who had chosen the cash option were stranded in the capital, where the presence of massive numbers of UN personnel had caused prices to rocket.

Above: On the repatriation train.
Kompong Chhnang Province, Cambodia.

Right: War-lords on National Highway 12.
Kompong Thom Province, Cambodia.

124

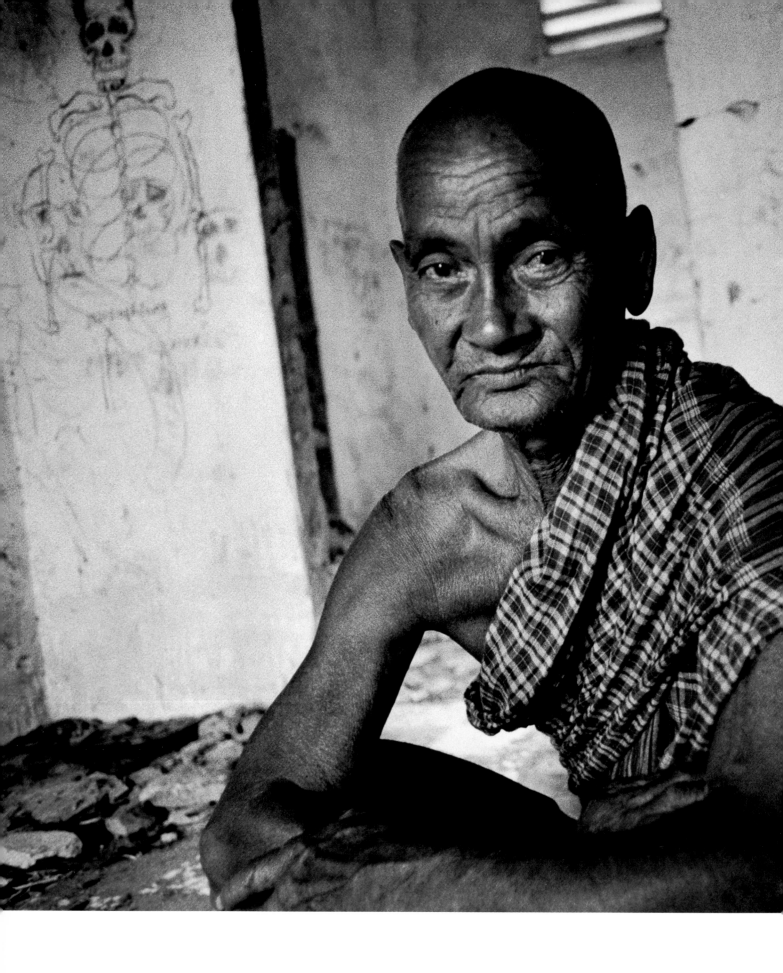

In a charnel house, a lay brother guards the remains of genocide victims recovered from nearby killing fields. Kompong Cham, Cambodia.

Buddhism and Marxism

In the Buddhist faith the soul cannot rest until there has been a proper burial. A great deal of thought has been given to the cremation of the skulls – between April 1975 and the end of 1978 an estimated one million people were killed by the Khmer Rouge or died of exhaustion and hunger. Cremation cannot take place until the pagodas where the ashes are to be buried have been repaired or rebuilt.

Cremation would destroy evidence, which would be welcomed by those responsible for the genocide, in the course of which eight thousand bonzes (members of the priesthood) were also murdered.

Left: Camp for internally displaced people under the hill pagoda of Phnom Sampou. Battambang Province, Cambodia.

Right: Waiting for the dry season. Siem Reap Province, Cambodia.

In the shadow of peace

When the monsoon ends in winter, Phnom Penh starts its annual dry-season offensive against the Khmer Rouge, promising that the marginalized jungle rebels will finally be crushed. They are rebels without a cause and their nocturnal looting and occasional explosive attacks on Cambodia's two railway lines serve mainly to frighten off potential investors and unsettle the local population.

But in this fragile peace all the parties want the closeness and protection of the ancient holy places.

The new royal troops are camped around Angkor Wat, the national symbol. The Banteay Srei temple, far away in the jungle, has been mined from the inside by the troops, from the outside by the Khmer Rouge. At dusk the building, regarded as the finest example of Khmer architecture, changes its guardians.

Once again Preah Vihear can only be reached via Thailand. The temple, perched on the edge of the rocky slopes of the Damrak range, is held by the Khmer Rouge forces; remote-controlled mines have been laid on the steep access route in the Cambodian jungle. Hundreds of attacking government soldiers were killed in 1994 attempting to climb it.

When danger threatens, the population pitch camp near the pagodas. Flight, internal expulsion and mines are the daily reality and fate, 'dharma', of the rural people in divided Cambodia.

Above and right: Mine victims, the blind and the handicapped, in a stadium where an American evangelist is selling healing in exchange for souls. Phnom Penh, Cambodia.

False promises

The international community had to restore peace in Cambodia because it is in the region of the world with the fastest growing economies.

Once before, in 1865 when it was in danger of disappearing between Vietnam and Siam (now Thailand), the country was saved for exploitation: it became a French protectorate.

The huge UN mission in 1992–1993 brought the country very little hope of sustained development.

Within a short time the government succumbed to every possible form of corruption.

In the well-established Cambodian tradition, its representatives' first priority was to protect themselves against the people with armed squads. And when drought threatened in the countryside the people came thronging to the city, in the belief that the minister with the mobile phone would actually pass their desperate cry for rain on to heaven.

In the house of God

Pagodas, monasteries and temples are not only religious meeting places and sites chosen and reserved for spiritual contemplation, they also express and foster the community's identity.

In Vietnam, Confucian ideology allowed the state to influence all aspects of life and the priests exercised more control than was possible elsewhere. When the Socialist Republic was proclaimed after the country's reunification in 1975, all ecclesiastical matters were brought under government control.

In 1981 a government-backed church replaced the Unified Buddhist Church of Vietnam and now, when more and more people are flocking to temples and churches, its priests are going on hunger strike and agitating for its reinstatement. Vietnam's economic upswing has led to greater tolerance by the government but not yet to religious freedom.

After 1975 state-controlled orphanages and other welfare institutions were handed back to the mostly Christian orders, mainly through lack of funds.

But in the Confucian temple holistic treatment is now available again. Thich Tân Câu, an eighty-year-old monk, studied Buddhism from 1950 to 1953 in Calcutta, where he acquired his knowledge of acupuncture. Since returning to Hanoi, where he also spent the war years, he treats several dozen patients a day in the courtyard of a small pagoda. While a woman suffering from chronic migraine meditates, fourteen-year-old Bui Tiên Dong, crippled by meningitis, tests the strength he has regained after a year's treatment.

Above: In the Wat Ounalom. Phnom Penh, Cambodia.

Left: In Dien Huu pagoda. Hanoi, Vietnam.

No 'Middle Way'

The Shwedagon pagoda, said to be 2,500 years old, is one of the holiest in the Buddhist world. Since the Anglo-Burmese wars it has always been an important scene of political events in the country's recent history. A conflagration in 1931 was an omen of the years of depression and protests against British rule.

Aung San Suu Kyi, winner of the Nobel Peace Prize in 1991, gave the most important speech in her election campaign here during a general strike on 26 August 1988, calling for an end to violence and the restoration of human rights based on multi-party democracy. The landslide victory of her National League for Democracy in these first-ever free elections was afterwards completely ignored by the military regime and the elections were annulled. Aung San Suu Kyi was released from six years' house arrest in the summer of 1995, and although her freedom of movement is still severely curtailed by the junta, she is now trying to rebuild her shattered party.

In releasing her from house arrest the government had not had a change of heart; it was demonstrating its self-confidence and trying to improve its image, mainly in order to join ASEAN (Association of South East Asian Nations).

Religion and resistance

Vietnam's religion is a mixture of Mahayana Buddhism and ancestor worship. It existed long before the adoption, in the thousand years of Chinese colonization (111 BC to 938 AD), of the '*mingfeng*', the Confucian value system which governed the structure of the family and became the state orthodoxy in independent Vietnam, especially in the 14th and 15th centuries.

Taoism also came from the north to the 'pacified south'. This gave the resident farming population such figures as the Jade Emperor Ngoc Hoang and such systems as geomancy and horoscopes, which helped them understand the connections between nature and the cosmos.

But Taoism also encouraged hero worship, introducing a political element into Vietnam's religion, which became more and more important as time went by. First of all it was the resistance fighters against the Chinese, who were raised to divine status, and then figures like Nguyen Trung Truc, who set fire to the French warship *Espérance*, surrendered to the colonial authorities in exchange for civilian hostages and was executed in 1868. Thich Quang Duc's famous self-immolation in the lotus position on 11 June 1963 was a protest against the Diem regime and the USA which supported it.

Above: Novices on the way up to the Shwedagon pagoda. Rangoon, Burma.

Above right: Religious worship in front of the statue of the resistance fighter Nguyen Trung Truc. Rach Gia, Kien Giang Province, Vietnam.

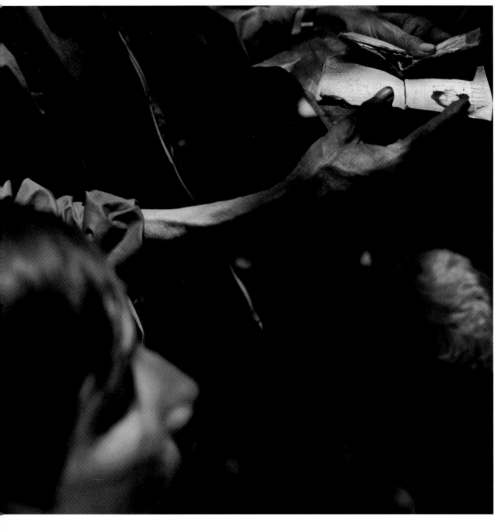

Exodus

In the spring of 1993, in the run-up to the elections under the UN mandate in Cambodia, Vietnamese fishermen were massacred on the 'Great Lake'. The Khmer Rouge – having pulled out of the peace process, claiming that Vietnam had never withdrawn all its troops and that thousands of Vietnamese were still living under cover in Cambodia – were hoping to exploit the latent anti-Vietnamese feeling in Cambodia.

30,000 ethnic Vietnamese who had lived on the 'Great Lake' for generations broke up their floating villages and the convoys of houseboats glided down the Tonle Sap, past Phnom Penh and along the Bassac river towards the Vietnamese border.

A group of six thousand people who did not get across the border were used for months as a political football between the Phnom Penh government elected in the meantime, which was trying to prevent the return of the stranded people to their ancestral home through new, ethnically discriminatory laws, and Hanoi, which wanted to cover up their refusal of entry.

During a visit by the Special Representative of the Secretary General for Human Rights in Cambodia, the refugees produced documents – identity cards, passports and tax forms from the sixties – as proof of their Cambodian residence. They also sent King Sihanouk a letter asking for permission to return to the lake. Under the protection of the *Samdech Euv*, the king-father, they would put all their effort into helping to rebuild Cambodia.

The way to purification

According to the legend, the Buddha gave a hermit a hair while passing his grotto. The hermit kept the hair until Tissa, an 11th-century king, asked him for it.

Tissa, the son of an alchemistic sorcerer and a Naga princess, fulfilled the condition that the relic should be kept in a shrine, or stupa, which was to be built on a rock resembling the hermit's skull, with the help of Thagyamin, the king of the *nats*. These 37 spirits, worshipped in Burma, helped to carry the block lying on the bottom of the Gulf of Martaban to the summit of the Paunglaung mountain range, over 1,000 metres high, in a mythical ship.

The pilgrimage through the jungle from the sea up to the pagoda, a journey of several hours, is a must for all Burma's Buddhists. Over the years the bricked-up stupa and the hanging rocks have become completely covered with their offerings of gold leaf.

Monk on the Bay of Bengal. Chaungtha,
Irrawaddy, Burma.

The propagation of the teachings

In 629 the young monk Hsüan Tsang set
out for the west from the capital of the
Chinese Tang dynasty (now Xian) to seek
the law that the Buddha had bequeathed to
the world. Seventeen years later he returned
with 657 Sanskrit scrolls on a frame and
devoted the rest of his life to deciphering,
translating and teaching them.

This transfer of religion, whose effects
reached as far as Korea and Japan, led to
a whole series of pilgrimages to the sacred
places on the Ganges. Not all those who set
out returned home.

The monk I Tsing (634–713) wrote:
*'There were some who crossed the Great
Wall and went west alone; others, also
unaccompanied, who crossed the wide
ocean. Not one of them that did not have
all his thoughts on the sacred trail; all were
carried along by the belief that one day they
would return in possession of the four
blessings. Only a few reached their goal.
They were prevented by the immense stony
deserts in the land of the elephants [India],
by the raging rivers and pitiless sun, the flood
waves, whipped up by giant fish, the crests
and troughs of the waves, foaming up to the
sky. As solitary wanderers they roamed behind
the Iron Towers [between Samarkand and
Bukhara] between ten thousand mountains,
plunged down steep chasms and were
smashed to pieces in the depths. Beyond
the copper pillars [south of Tonkin], as sailors
thrown back on their own resources, they lost
their lives when crossing the thousand deltas.
Of the fifty who set out, only a handful
survived.'*

From the epilogue by Ulf Diederichs to René Grousset,
Die Reise nach Westen, Eugen Diederichs Verlag,
Munich, 1986, p. 250 (German edition of *Sur les
Traces du Bouddha*, Plon, Paris, 1929.)

4

Deltopolis

Angkor in the 13th Century

THE WALLED CITY

The wall of the city is some five miles in circumference. It has five gates, each with double portals. Two gates pierce the eastern side; the other sides have one gate only. Outside the wall stretches a great moat, across which access to the city is given by massive causeways. Flanking the causeways on each side are fifty-four divinities resembling war-lords in stone, huge and terrifying. All five gates are similar. The parapets of the causeways are of solid stone, carved to represent nine-headed serpents. The fifty-four divinities grasp the serpents with their hands, seemingly to prevent their escape. Above each gate are grouped five gigantic heads of Buddha, four of them facing the four cardinal points of the compass, the fifth head, brilliant with gold, holds a central position. On each side of the gates are elephants, carved in stone.

CAMBODIAN DWELLINGS

The Royal Palace, as well as official buildings and homes of the nobles, all face the east. The Royal Palace stands to the north of the Golden Tower and the Bridge of Gold; starting from the gate its circumference is nearly one and a half miles. The tiles of the central dwelling are of lead; other parts of the palace are covered with pottery tiles, yellow in color. Lintels and columns, all decorated with carved or painted Buddhas, are immense. The roofs, too, are impressive. Long colonnades and open corridors stretch away, interlaced in harmonious relation. In the chamber where the sovereign attends to affairs of state, there is a golden window, with mirrors disposed on square columns to the right and left of the window-trim, forty or so in number. Below the window is a frieze of elephants. I have heard it said that within the palace are many marvellous sights, but these are so strictly guarded that I had no chance to see them....

The dwellings of the princes and holders of high office are wholly different in size and design from those of the people. The family temple and the main hall are covered with tiles; all the outlying buildings are thatched with straw. The rank of every official determines the size of his house.

Straw thatch covers the dwellings of the commoners, not one of whom would dare place the smallest bit of tile on his roof. In this class, too, wealth determines the size of the house, but no one would venture to vie with the nobility.

Preceding pages: View across the Huangpu. Shanghai, China.

The cost of growth

In the People's Republic, one third of the population of 1.2 thousand million lives in the delta of the Yangtze, China's longest river. 13 million residents and millions of migrant workers make Shanghai one of the most densely poulated megacities in the world.

Between 1990 and 1993 the world's longest and third longest suspension bridges were built across the Huangpu, the Yangtze's last tributary before the China Sea. On the east bank, opposite the 'Bund', Shanghai's commercial district in the twenties, the Pudong finance, business and export zone is being developed; from here China's economy is to be controlled in the next century, the Asian-Pacific century.

The planners also invoked the traditional image of the dragon to gain approval from the People's Congress for the eventual use of the Yangtze. With the megacity at its head, the winding river will open up an economic area which, after the completion of the biggest hydroelectric power station in the world at the 'Three Gorges', planned for 2009, will extend as far as Chongqing, 1,400 kilometres from the river mouth. 10,000-tonne ocean-going ships will anchor there. The new reservoir behind the 185-metre-high dam, already referred to by Mao Zedong in a poem in 1956, will flood over 100 cultural monuments and the homes of 1.4 million people.

A lack of harmony between heaven, earth and the human race now signifies not that a dynasty may collapse but that the limits of new growth have been exceeded.

Quarrymen's children under the Kaspur bridge. Dhaka, Bangladesh.

IMMIGRANTS

Chinese sailors coming to the country note with pleasure that it is not necessary to wear clothes, and, since rice is easily had, women easily persuaded, houses easily run, furniture easily come by, and trade easily carried on, a great many sailors desert to take up permanent residence.

Zhou Daguan, *The Customs of Cambodia* (1296–1297), trans. from the French version by Paul Pelliot (1902) of Zhou Daguan's Chinese original by J. Gilman d'Arcy Paul, The Siam Society under Royal Patronage, Bangkok, 1992, pp. 2, 5, 69.

Foreign Merchants in the Bay of Bengal

Owing largely to the Portuguese trade, Chittagong had become a commercial centre by the end of the 16th century and had acquired from the Portuguese the name of Porto Grande or the great port as distinguished from Satgaon (Hoogly, West Bengal) which was known [as] Porto Piqueno or the little port, the two ports being regarded as situated on the eastern and western branches of the Ganges. This importance it owed to its easy access, its safe anchorage and its position near the mouth of the Meghna which was the principal route to the Royal Capital.

'Chittagong District Gazetteer', Chittagong [n.d.], in *East Pakistan District Gazetteer*, Government of East Pakistan, 1970, pp. 73–74.

They were not lawful subjects of the king of Portugal and owned no allegiance to the Portuguese viceroy at Goa. They also did not fully submit to the authority of the Arakanese king, though they owed much to his favour in having strong settlements at Deanga (Chittagong) and Syrium in his dominion. The Arakanese king was often incensed by their piratical raids and had to be harsh with them, but the differences were as quickly composed as they arose; for, the Arakanese king in his bid to check the Muslim rulers of Bengal could hardly do without them. This historical fact was of immense import in explaining the reason for the Portuguese supremacy in Chittagong. The Arakanese were equally noted for their skill in navigation and river fighting. Their alliance with the Portuguese for political reasons soon developed into an unholy comradeship in arms for carrying on plundering raids into the coastal territories and riverine tracts of lower and East Bengal as far up as Hoogly in West Bengal and Dacca the capital city of Bengal. With small and light half-galleys called galleasses they surprised and carried off whole villages and harried the poor villagers from their assemblies, their market places, festivals and weddings,

Floating crane lifted on to the quayside by the cyclone in Patenga harbour. Chittagong, Bangladesh.

143

seizing as slaves both men and women, perpetrating strange cruelties and burning all that they could not carry away. The Portuguese sold off their captives while the Arakanese employed them in agriculture and other domestic services. These depradatory raids continued for well over one hundred years from the middle of the 16th century up to the Mughal conquest of Chittagong....

The Mughal administrators did not pay much attention to the growth and development of the port. The international trade was then carried on exclusively by the Dutch, French and English who established their factories at Dacca, Hoogly and Calcutta and were fighting among themselves for supremacy. Nevertheless, these European traders had their agencies in Chittagong which continued to be an important mart for supplying cotton, timber, rice, spices, salt and other commodities.... Among the European traders the English emerged, after long competition with others, as the most successful and the East India Company in the wake of their commercial enterprise became the master of Chittagong in 1760.

'Chittagong District Gazetteer', Chittagong [n.d.], in *East Pakistan District Gazetteer*, Government of East Pakistan, 1970, pp. 259–61.

Journey to Rangoon in the 19th Century

It was at daybreak on the 2nd of April, 1871, that we—an English friend was with me—first saw the shores of Burma. We had been a short time at sea, having left Madras eight days previously, but the end of the voyage was none the less welcome, for it was about the season that the monsoon changes, and those terrific revolving storms called cyclones sweep the upper part of the Bay of Bengal, so often with fatal effect....

We enjoyed a remarkably pleasant voyage. Masulipatam was reached on the second day.... Leaving Bimlipatam—a simple cluster of mud huts—we saw nothing but sky and water until the lighthouse on the Alguada reef, fifteen or twenty miles distant from Cape Negrais (the south-west extremity of Pegu), rose up from the ocean's bed before us. It is erected on a very dangerous reef, more than a mile in length, and much of which is only just above water at low tide. The shaft, built of red stone, is 160 feet in height, and, no land being in sight, certainly presented a most singular appearance; however, with our binoculars we could distinguish two or three lines of billows dashing themselves one after another upon the dark rocks.

Repatriation of Khmer refugees on Mekong ships. Phnom Penh, Cambodia.

Soon after 'sighting' the land we received on board the pilot, and then half an hour's steaming brought us to the mouth of the Rangoon river, with its low, wooded shores, and red obelisks on either headland—warnings to the mariner. Sandbanks, whose edges are marked by large iron buoys indicating the channel's bed, stretched for a long distance out to sea. We passed a dozen or more large ships before reaching the river's mouth; these, the captain informed us, anchored there in order to free themselves from the port dues to which they would be subject if lying at the city, and the masters go 'up to town' and engage their cargoes. At its entrance the Rangoon river is two miles in width, while opposite the city, twenty-six miles above, it narrows to about a third of a mile, with four or five fathoms' depth. The foreign ships anchored in the river made a very considerable show, our visit being at the height of the rice season. Rangoon, lying upon level ground, extends for about a mile along the river, and perhaps three times that distance inland. By the bank of the river there runs a broad macadamised street, called 'the Strand', and facing this are the Government offices and many imposing and substantial stores and dwelling-houses. The city abounds with rich tropical foliage, which shades many of the teak and bamboo built huts, and from the steamer's deck we can see a small English cantonment, two or three European churches, and several large pagodas, with gilded and richly ornamented spires. Beyond the city we see a jungle of palms and bananas, and bamboos stretching away, a waving sea of green, to the very horizon itself. The country about Rangoon—the delta of the great Irrawaddy river—is of much the same nature as the *embouchure* of the Ganges, being low, sandy, and muddy, and subject to tremendous floods in the rainy season.

Frank Vincent, *The Land of the White Elephant: Sights and Scenes in South-Eastern Asia. A Personal Narrative of Travel and Adventure in Farther India, Embracing the Countries of Burma, Siam, Cambodia, and Cochin-China*, 1871–2, Low, Marston, Low and Searle, London, 1873, pp. 1–4.

From the Sacred City to the Commercial City

Rangoon came into British hands in 1852, and at the time possessed no commerce worthy of the name, indeed it was only known as the place for pilgrims to the Shwe Dagôn pagoda to stay at, and the residence of the Regent of Pegu, as being the guard station on the most accessible mouth of the Irrawaddy. Ten years later, ships entered or cleared from the port having a tonnage of 295,000 tons, and the imports were worth £1,200,000, the

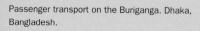

Passenger transport on the Buriganga. Dhaka, Bangladesh.

145

exports £1,400,000, and since that date—a year or two after Mandalay had been founded—the tonnage has increased to 1,000,000, the value of the imports to £5,000,000 sterling, and the exports to £4,000,000. In a quarter of a century the commerce of British Burma rose to nearly £20,000,000 sterling. The population has quadrupled; public works are carried on; education is widely disseminated; the administration is carefully managed by British officials; a railway, 163 miles long, has been made; there are 1300 miles of telegraph lines; stately law courts and other public buildings have sprung up, and so far from the work being a tax on the Indian Imperial Treasury, British Burma has been, after its first few years, more than self-supporting. For a considerable time it has contributed to the Imperial Treasury a clear surplus of a million sterling. The mere figures are in themselves surprising, but they cannot be truly appreciated unless they are read alongside the obvious, undeniable, and acknowledged prosperity and contentment of the native population. Since the annexation of Upper Burma these figures have been roughly multiplied by ten, and there is a steady yearly increase which would be greater if Burma were allowed to make use of her yearly surpluses.

As long as there was a king of Burma, Mandalay was a larger town than Rangoon and an infinitely more picturesque one. It still remains by a long way the second town in Burma, but Rangoon has over-passed it in population.

Shway Yoe (Sir J.G. Scott), *The Burman: His Life and Notions* (1882), rev. edn, Macmillan, London, 1910, pp. 539–40.

The village and the countryside were the characteristic focuses of Western-inspired economic development; they were the production sites for primary produce and resources. Change, however, affected not only the sites of production, but also the places from which production was directed, the newly developed colonial capitals and Bangkok. Under the new régime of Western-inspired production and trade, the two great tasks of cities were commerce and territorial administration, combined in ways that had never previously been possible in Southeast Asia. The cities of the high colonial period possessed, unlike their classical antecedents, the skills and technology to marry both these functions effectively....

In 1930, there were sixteen cities with populations of 100,000 or more. They can be divided into three groups: first, the 'old' indigenous capitals of Mandalay, Bangkok, Hanoi, Yogyakarta and Surakarta, mostly modelled on the principles of the old sacred city; second, old colonial cities with their origins in the merchant capital era of Western presence, cities founded

Transporting prisoners in the Old City. Dhaka, Bangladesh.

or settled by Westerners essentially as trading posts: Batavia, Semarang, Surabaya, Manila, Penang and Singapore; third, the new colonial cities of Rangoon, Saigon, Kuala Lumpur, Palembang and Bandung, cities which owed their importance to being sites of the commercial expansion which marked this period of high colonialism. Comparing this freeze-frame to one taken a century or so before reveals a number of crucial developments. Pre-eminence had passed from the old sacred city to the city based on commerce—Mandalay gave way to Rangoon, Yogyakarta to Batavia, Hué to Saigon....

More spectacular than this change in the functions of cities was the late, rapid increase in their sizes. Before the last part of the nineteenth century, urban populations in Southeast Asia generally grew more slowly than rural ones, a reflection of the limited, perhaps stultifying, effect of Western merchant capital on urban development. The development of state territorial control and more pervasive forms of economic activity, however, saw the beginnings of rapid and continuing urbanization; now all the major cities grew in population much faster than the rural areas that surrounded them, partly because of relatively poor conditions in the local (and international) countryside, and partly because the city seemed to promise a better life of expanding economic opportunities.

Robert E. Elson, 'International Commerce, the State and Society: Economic and Social Change/Aspects of Social Change', in Nicholas Tarling (ed.), *Cambridge History of Southeast Asia*, vol. II, *The Nineteenth and Twentieth Centuries*, Cambridge University Press, Cambridge, 1992, pp. 168–69.

From the Village to the Urban Centre

Child hawkers and labourers are on the increase in [Borguna] with the influx of floating people.... According to a rough official estimate, about 2,000 children aging 5 to 12 have been engaged in manual jobs for eking out their livelihood.

Of the total, 1000 are hawkers and the remaining work on daily wage or work as the helping hands of masons, hotels, restaurants, bidi factories, motorgarages, bicycle repairing shops, welding workshops and brickfields. Many others are also working as rickshawpullers and domestic servants. These children have trekked to the town areas along with their families who were rendered shelterless either by erosion or recurring flooding and other

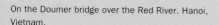

On the Doumer bridge over the Red River. Hanoi, Vietnam.

147

natural calamities and eventually were forced to abandon their respective village home in quest of work for bare survival.

The Daily Star, Dhaka, 22 January 1992.

A fire which raged through a slum area of Dhaka killed at least five people, injured more than 70 and left more than 10,000 homeless, Bangladeshi police said on Tuesday.

They said the blaze broke out on Monday evening in the capital's Islamabad district, home to nearly 15,000 people, and took hundreds of firefighters six hours to put out....

Rescuers are still sifting through rubble for other victims, they said.

Rubbish dumps and abandoned canals surrounding the slum hampered firefighters, witnesses said.

'It (the slum) can be reached only through a few bamboo poles placed across the canals, to serve as bridges and hardly one man can pass over at a time,' said a resident of the nearby Lalbagh area....

Most of the slum people came to the city after floods, cyclones or river erosion destroyed their homes in rural villages.

Working People's Daily, Rangoon, 12 March 1992.

Towards the Megacity

In discussing the history of the city in South Asia an important distinction must be drawn between 'urban growth' (an increase in the size of cities and towns) and 'urbanization' (an increase in the percentage of the total population living in cities and towns). Urban growth is a phenomenon which can be seen throughout the history of South Asia, but urbanization is a decidedly recent phenomenon, restricted largely to the last two centuries and most especially to the post-Independence period.

Karl J. Schmidt, *An Atlas and Survey of South Asian History*, M.E. Sharpe, New York, 1995, p. 134.

United Nations predictions paint a stunning portrait of urban life in Asia in 2010: 30 Asian cities will have populations greater than 5 million (compared with only two US cities and six in Europe). Shanghai and Bombay will each have 20 million people. Beijing, Dhaka, Jakarta, Manila, Tianjin, Calcutta and Delhi will have more than 15 million.

John Naisbitt, *Megatrends Asia: The Eight Asian Megatrends That Are Changing The World*, Nicholas Brealey Publishing Ltd, London, 1995, 1996, pp. 145–46. Reprinted with the permission of Simon & Schuster from *Megatrends Asia* by John Naisbitt. Copyright © 1996 by Megatrend Limited.

Monument to the Cultural Revolution on the Yangtze bridge. Nanjing, China.

Behind the gleaming skyscrapers of Asia's major cities is another reality: the slums and squatter settlements that are home to hundreds of millions of Asians. Both the shanties and the skyscrapers are symptomatic of the unwillingness or inability of governments and markets to deal with land as a central force in shaping the quality of city life.

Yok-shiu F. Lee, 'To Make Asia Livable', *Newsweek International*, 9 May 1994, p. 43.

Even the greatest and most enduring cities seem vulnerable when one considers the natural, political, and economic upheavals they must contend with. Poverty, unemployment, disease, crime, and pollution have plagued urban centers for 10,000 years, since the earliest cities developed around granaries and armories in Mesopotamia and Anatolia. There is reason to believe, however, that while the individual problems facing cities are not new, an unholy synergy created in the developing world when explosive population growth, industrialization, and capital scarcity meet means dangers on an unprecedented scale.

Eugene Linden, 'The Exploding Cities of the Developing World', *Foreign Affairs*, vol. 75, no. 1, January/February 1996, p. 56.

The excerpt reprinted by permission of *Foreign Affairs*. Copyright 1996 by the Council of Foreign Relations, Inc.

Asleep on the Yangtze. Nanjing, China.

A monsoon storm blows dust clouds across the central market. Phnom Penh, Cambodia.

A changing city

Cambodia's old capital, Angkor, declined after 1430 when Khmer policy began to turn away from the rice monoculture and to seek to create wealth through the production of goods and trade. Phnom Penh developed as a maritime trans-shipment point where the Tonle Sap flows into the Mekong and the Bassac arm separates from the river. Early travellers could not believe that the rulers of such a modest place were descendants of the kings of Angkor.

Phnom Penh, unlike other Southeast Asian cities such as Bangkok, did not become a 'primate city', a colonial megacity several times larger than the old royal capital which it had superseded and in which a large part of the country's population lived – which is paradoxical in view of the precolonial idea that the capital was the nation.

The tragedy of Phnom Penh, the most beautiful city in what was Indochina, began after 1970 when Cambodia was dragged into the Vietnam war. Its population of half a million rose to two million with the stream of displaced persons. After 17 April 1975 Phnom Penh, like the other urban centres, was evacuated by the Khmer Rouge as part of their ultra-Marxist experiment and became a ghost town. It was only after Vietnam invaded and liberated it that the survivors returned from the countryside, began to repair their houses and flats or settle in ruined buildings that nobody claimed.

Political events since the early nineties have been reflected in the renaming of the streets: Boulevard Norodom (King), in honour of Sihanouk, used to be called Tousamouth, the *nom de guerre* of a former monk and activist in the Indochinese Communist party founded by Ho Chi Minh. In the Second World War the party fought against the French colonial administration which collaborated with Japan. Boulevard USSR became Boulevard Pochentong after the international airport.

Above: Street children. Ho Chi Minh City, Vietnam.

Right: Blocks of flats built in the sixties. Phnom Penh, Cambodia.

A shortage of clean water, or polluted water and unhygienic living conditions, can cause blindness resulting from the infectious disease trachoma or from onchocercosis spread by mosquito bites, which is common near rivers. Lack of vitamin A is another common cause of blindness, especially in children.

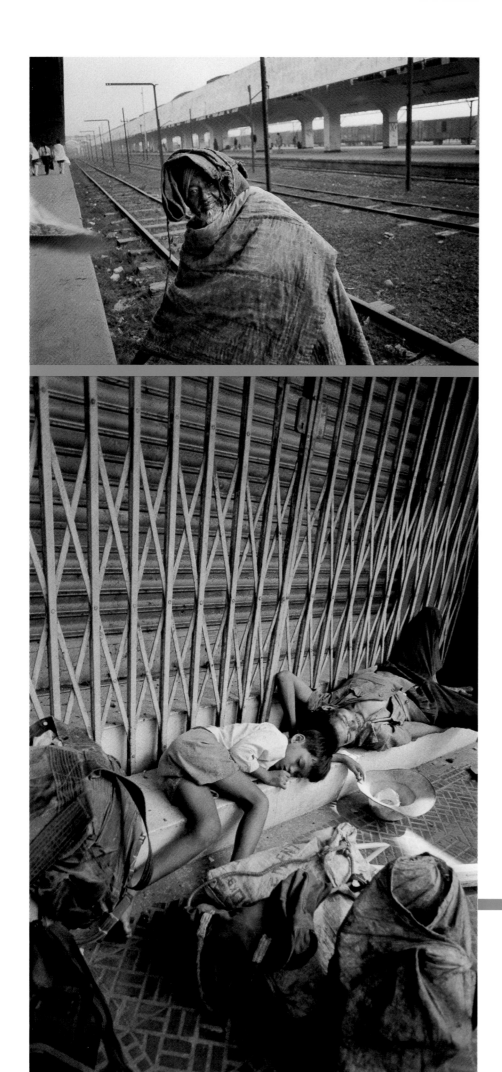

Above: Quarrel in a homeless family. Dhaka, Bangladesh.

Top left: A man living in the sidings behind Kamalpur station starts his casual job as a porter. Dhaka, Bangladesh.

Left: Rural migrants after arriving in the centre of Ho Chi Minh City, Vietnam.

The way out of the crisis

The decision to move to the city is a decision taken within the family or clan. The journey is made in several stages and goes through rural villages and urban centres to known meeting-points on the edge of the capitals; from here the way leads to plots in the administrative and commercial centres that are often left empty because of land speculation.

The occupation of this land starts with fragile *kutcha* homes with walls made of thatch and sheets of plastic. As time goes by, these are replaced by more solid, *pukka* structures with clay or brick walls and corrugated iron. If no paid arsonists or bulldozers arrive on the scene, the houses become settlements with a village-like social structure. These settlements, although called slums and seen by outsiders as places of poverty, are the symbol of a more secured existence.

Political will can legalize these settlements and thereby provide new arrivals with a base from which they can discover and take over for themselves what governments have created, often mainly to enhance the state's prestige: the best medical care in the country, the most expensive educational establishments, the most efficient transport systems, the most important ministerial buildings – in other words the incentives for business and industry to establish themselves and create jobs. The urban migrants then talk about this when they go back to their villages on a visit and encourage others to follow.

Behind the bamboo curtain

In the last few years the Burmese State Law and Order Restoration Council has assigned the navy to protect the 150,000-square-kilometre economic zone in the Andaman Sea. Here French and American firms are developing natural gas fields for the Burmese Myanmar Oil and Gas Enterprise, which will be linked to a new refinery southwest of Bangkok by a pipeline under the sea and across country.

For its help in keeping the Rangoon government in power over the years, China is being allowed to develop a small Burmese fishing port in the Irrawaddy delta into its gateway to the Indian Ocean.

Pilgrim ships will probably still be able to pass through this new 'heart of darkness' once a year, since the *tatmadaw*, Burma's armed forces, are made up of devout Buddhists. But never before in Burma's history have the generals exercised such strong control over politics and business.

Left: Excavation of the harbour basin for the Chinese submarine base at Hainggyi island. Irrawaddy delta, Burma.

Right: Military police outside an obscure financial institution. Phnom Penh, Cambodia.

Below right: Soldier at the gate of the Aung San stadium, the finish of the annual marathon, which even children have to take part in. Rangoon, Burma.

Street sweepers waiting in the monsoon rain. Rangoon, Burma.

Top and above: Settlement of ecological refugees on the Buriganga river. Imamganj district of Dhaka, Bangladesh.

At home on the street

City dwellers in developing countries are the fastest growing section of the population worldwide.

In 1972 Dhaka had a few thousand inhabitants, the same number as at the beginning of the 19th century, when Calcutta became the centre for the British Raj.

By 1994 the city already had a population of 7.5 million. The growth reflects the economic development of the country, which influences migration, both voluntary and enforced. By the year 2000 it is estimated that Dhaka will have 12.2 million inhabitants.

In Dhaka today, more than two-thirds of the total population – the poor and the lower middle classes – are crowded into one-third of the habitable area. In Calcutta illegal residents account for 44 per cent of the city's population. Half a million of the poorest have no alternative but to live and die on the pavement.

Above: Street children at a free lesson on Sadarghat
pier in the harbour. Dhaka, Bangladesh.

Education for girls, who would otherwise be
discriminated against on religious grounds, is
promoted by UNICEF and non-governmental
organizations. Dropout rates are much lower than in
the state schools, where the cost of books and uniform
often forces parents to remove their children early.

The Gonoshahajjo schools, for example, charge
a nominal fee of one taka – 2.5 US cents. The
organization started with two primary schools in 1986
and since the early nineties has set up more than 150
new schools a year. It builds the school, a three-room
structure laid out for 180 children in two shifts, and

the local authority provides the land. Entrance can
be at any age.

Pupils are also taught about the law – particularly
important when they are often self-employed and
working on the fringes of legality or are exploited
by others.

Left: A boy resting next to leather remnants and toxic waste in the tanneries in Hazaribagh. Dhaka, Bangladesh.

Leather is an important element in Bangladesh's export trade. The skins are bleached and coloured with sulphuric and nitric acid and carcinogenic cromosol, which is not easily degradable. The chemicals go straight into the Buriganga river and the water at the points where the effluent is discharged no longer contains any oxygen.

Because of the existing plants, dating from the fifties, or lack of funds, it is not possible to move the tanneries away from Dhaka to where a central disposal system could be built. The move would also jeopardize competitiveness on the international market, since legal standards for environmental protection and the health of the workforce would have to be met and this would increase production costs.

Left: In the Kulipaltti slum at Kamalpur station, drinking water and water for all domestic and sanitary uses is drawn from a single plastic pipe which emerges from the ground at the lowest point of the muddy area. Dhaka, Bangladesh.

Water only appears to be plentiful in the countries of Southeast Asia, and safe water is even less so. In Cambodia only 7 per cent of the population have access to drinking water; in rural Burma, 30 per cent.

In Bangladesh 80 per cent of the population live less than 150 metres from a tube well. With this coverage it is ahead of all other developing countries.

Above: In a monsoon shower. Dhaka, Bangladesh.

In the street

In 1993 all minors had to leave the textile factories in Bangladesh following a campaign against child labour by the US Congress. There they had at least been in the care of their mothers and had helped with light work on the manufacture of casual wear. Having been thrown out, they then had to earn their contribution to the family income breaking bricks, which was hard and less well paid. Others joined the children selling garlands of fresh jasmine at petrol stations.

Or they disappeared in the walled old city quarter of Roth Khola and other centres of prostitution on the edge of town.

The art of city life

Shanghai's population will rise from 13 million in 1992 to 17 million by the year 2000, Calcutta's from 11.8 to 15.7 million.

A rise on this scale does not allow organic development. Growth takes place in a constant balancing act between vitality and chaos. The situation encourages competition and alienation from nature, innovation and corruption, wealth and exploitation, culture and sickness.

City life is reduced to the art of survival.

Right: Passers-by outside Sealdah station. Calcutta, West Bengal, India.

Below: Investors crowding round a stock exchange at night, watching prices on the screen. Shanghai, China.

Top: Fugitives from the countryside leaving their flooded
tents on the edge of Calcutta. West Bengal, India.

Above: Clearing-up operations after the 1991 floods.
Wuxi, Jiangsu Province, China.

Right: Raising the protective dykes on Tai Hu Lake
during the 1991 flood. Yixing, Jiangsu Province, China.

Tyranny of the absolute

China built its Great Wall to keep out the uncontrollable nomadic tribes beyond its borders. It built the Great Canal, the longest in the world, to avoid the uncertainties of the limitless expanse and mystery of the sea. 1,800 kilometres long, running parallel to the coast, it has provided a link between the capital Beijing and the rice-growing areas in the Yangtze delta since the end of the 13th century.

Although the Yellow River has shifted several times, the canal has always remained open to traffic. In 1495 alone 200,000 men were mustered to work on it.

In the light of the hundred-year project under construction in the 'Three Gorges', the increasing frequency of the heavy floods in the Yangtze basin in the nineties portends a catastrophe still not officially acknowledged by Beijing.

In 1975 Henan Province was hit by three typhoons in a month. The iron dams built in the fifties from Soviet plans held for two days, then 62 burst in a single night, including two of China's biggest iron dams on the Huai river, the largest tributary of the Yangtze. The number of victims was between 86,000 and 230,000. Two million were cut off for months and eleven million suffered from epidemics and hunger.

Above and right: A mother and child and a group of boys look for usable waste on the Tonle Sap promenade and along the route of the dustcart. Phnom Penh, Cambodia.

Above and right: Road surfacing and excavation work, using corvée labour, on the edge of the city. Rangoon, Burma.

After 1988 Burma's military government began to create a vacuum in the centre of Rangoon which, in line with the name changes all over the country, had been renamed Yangon, 'City without Enemies'.

The populations of whole areas of the city, particularly those who had supported Aung San Suu Kyi's opposition party in the 1990 elections, were taken to wasteland outside the city, where they had to build wooden houses with limited materials while their tall, multi-storey town houses built in the thirties, often with shops attached, were seized by members of the armed forces and their families.

The camp-like satellite towns that emerged were connected by a ring road which even children helped to build. In 1991 Burma, under its new name Myanmar, signed the UN Convention on the Rights of the Child.

Top and above: On a rubbish dump. Ho Chi
Minh City, Vietnam.

Now that the commodities of war have been re-
used – steel from tanks and helicopters went
back to America in the form of Japanese cars –
the recycling of consumer goods has reached
Vietnam with the economic boom.

Bus passengers. Calcutta, West Bengal, India.

Delta
Country Profiles

Based on:

WESTLAKE, MICHAEL (ed.), *Far Eastern Economic Review*. Asia 1996 Yearbook, Hong Kong, 1996.

Additions from:

CHANDLER, DAVID P., *Brother Number One: A Political Biography of Pol Pot*, WestviewPress, Boulder 1992

KARNOW, STANLEY, *Vietnam: A History*, Penguin Books, New York, 1984

LINTNER, BERTIL, *Outrage: Burma's Struggle for Democracy*, White Lotus, Bangkok, 1990

NOVAK, JAMES J., *Bangladesh: Reflections on the Water*, Indiana University Press, Bloomington 1993

SCHMIDT, KARL J., *An Atlas and Survey of South Asian History*, M.E. Sharpe, London 1995

SWAIN, JON, *River of Time*, Heinemann, London, 1995

US DEPARTMENT OF STATE, *International Narcotics Control Strategy Report, March 1996, Southeast Asia and the Pacific*.

Bangladesh

On 15 August 1947 the British Raj ended and British India became independent. In the process of shaping two new dominions – Pakistan and India – Bengal was partitioned, and Muslim Bengal, which had most of the people, became East Pakistan while the Bengali Hindus got the western part of Bengal, which became an Indian province.

In December 1970, East Pakistan's Bangla-speaking Awami League leader, Sheikh Mujibur Rahman, gained a huge majority during an election and, over the protests of Urdu-speaking West Pakistan, stuck to his demand for regional autonomy. After talks between Mujib and President Yahya Khan broke down, in March 1971, Pakistan's army took control. India joined the war in early December and Bangladesh – the former East Pakistan – became independent. A new constitution was framed to establish Westminster-style parliamentary democracy and Mujib was swept back to power in March 1973. His government was toppled in a military coup on 15 August 1975, and Mujib was assassinated. Following a series of coups and assassinations, army chief of staff Lieutenant-General H.M. Ershad took over the presidency on 11 December 1983. He resigned from the army and was elected president on 15 October 1986. Ershad was deposed in December 1990 following anti-government protests, and was subsequently tried, convicted and jailed. Khaleda Zia became prime minister after a general election in February 1991. In September 1991, Bangladesh's constitution was amended to return the country to its Westminster-style governance, ending sixteen years of executive presidential rule.

In early 1996 a dispute broke out between Khaleda Zia and the centre-left opposition, led by Awami League President Sheikh Hasina Wajed, over general elections to be held under the auspices of a neutral caretaker government. After allegations of corruption and a series of anti-government strikes crippling the fragile economy and endangering the impoverished and overpopulated country's nascent democracy, Khaleda Zia was forced to resign on 30 March. A narrow victory in the new parliamentary elections held on 12 June brought back to power the Awami League with Sheikh Hasina Wajed following her father as prime minister twenty-five years after he had led the country into independence. Her election was crowned in December 1996 by the signing of a thirty-year agreement with India for sharing the waters of the Ganges, effectively resolving a source of conflict that had long soured relations between the two countries.

Burma

The Japanese occupation of 1942–1945 gave a group of young nationalists led by Aung San a chance to rise to political prominence. The Union of Burma was declared an independent republic on 4 January 1948, but immediately faced rebellions by communist groups and various ethnic minorities.

On 2 March 1962 the military, led by General Ne Win, seized power and ended a fourteen-year-long experiment with parliamentary democracy. The country then went into a self-imposed isolation. It became the Socialist Republic of the Union of Burma in 1974, and the economy continued to decline. Ne Win was succeeded as president by San Yu in 1981, but remained a chairman of the only legally permitted party, the Burmese Socialist Programme Party.

Ne Win and San Yu resigned from their respective posts in July 1988 amid mounting opposition against one-party rule and socialism. Nation-wide anti-government demonstrations rocked the country in August and September 1988. Hundreds of people were killed by troops in the capital. Eventually, the army formed the State Law and Order Restoration Council and assumed direct control of the state.

The new military government abolished the old socialist system and began to encourage free-market economy and foreign investment. It also organized a general election in May 1990, which led to a landslide victory for the main opposition party, the National League for Democracy. The elected assembly was never convened. NLD leader Aung San Suu Kyi remained under house arrest until July 1995. With her freedom of movement still severely restricted, Aung San Suu Kyi resumed making weekly speeches from the gate of her lakeside residence. However, sympathizers and members of the NLD who wanted to attend meetings inside the compound were being routinely detained. After the death in a Rangoon prison of the honorary consul to a number of Western countries, the international community again called for economic sanctions. Meanwhile the ruling junta has adopted the Indonesian model of 'dwifungsi' (dual function), which gives the armed forces an institutionalized role in political life. In 1996 Burma remained the world's largest producer of opium and heroin.

Cambodia

After France granted Cambodia independence in 1953, Prince Norodom Sihanouk sought to keep the country neutral in an effort to avoid being caught up in the war which engulfed Vietnam and Laos. In 1965 Sihanouk made secret arrangements with Vietnamese Communists, allowing them to station troops in Cambodia's east. On 18 March 1969 Nixon, then President of the United States, began the secret bombing of Cambodia which lasted until 14 August 1973.

Sihanouk was ousted in a coup in 1970 led by Lon Nol, which prompted him to form an alliance with the Khmer Rouge, a radical pro-Chinese guerrilla movement fighting the new US-backed government. On 17 April 1975 the Khmer Rouge, led by Pol Pot, captured Phnom Penh and established a radical agrarian society under which around one million people were killed or died of hunger, disease and overwork.

In late 1978, following two years of Khmer Rouge attacks across the Vietnamese border, Vietnam invaded Cambodia and set up a government in Phnom Penh headed by Khmer Rouge defectors and pro-Vietnamese communists. For the next thirteen years, a coalition, including the ousted Khmer Rouge and two non-communist resistance groups, continued to wage a guerrilla and mine war against the Vietnamese-backed regime in Phnom Penh.

On 23 October 1991, the four warring Cambodian factions signed a UN-sponsored peace agreement to set up a peace-keeping force to monitor the repatriation of the Khmer refugees from Thailand and the disarmament of the four armies, and to provide civilian personnel to monitor a transition period leading to free elections. In May 1993 the first multi-party election took place, and in September a new constitution was promulgated with Sihanouk as head of state. However, political instability and the military scene – including an active, although diminishing, Khmer Rouge insurgency – continued to overshadow the recovery of the country and favoured conditions under which Cambodia could transform into an offshore narco-state.

Vietnam

Ho Chi Minh declared Vietnam independent of French colonial rule on 2 September 1945 after Japan's surrender in World War II, but the French returned to rule the country until their defeat at Dien Bien Phu on 7 May 1954. Pending political settlement to be achieved through nationwide elections, the Geneva Accords divided Vietnam along a provisional demarcation line at the seventeenth parallel, establishing the Democratic People's Republic of Vietnam to the north and the Republic of Vietnam to the south.

In the ensuing years, fighting between the Soviet- and Chinese-supported communist North and the US-backed South intensified. In 1965 the United States committed its armed forces to defend the Republic of Vietnam, which was crumbling under the Vietcong insurgency supported by the North.

By 1968, when Hanoi launched the Tet offensive, more than 500,000 American troops were in Vietnam, American planes bombed Hanoi and Haiphong, and the CIA was engaged in a secret war in Laos against the communist Pathet Lao and the North Vietnamese.

In 1973 the Paris Peace Accords were signed, giving the US the diplomatic means of withdrawing its last forces. The war went on until the Republic of Vietnam, deprived of US bombing and logistical support, was defeated. Communist troops captured Saigon on 30 April 1975.

Unified as the Socialist Republic of Vietnam, the country's former two halves saw a massive exodus of 'boat people'. Facing a deteriorating economic situation and international isolation, Vietnam's communist party introduced free-market reforms in the late 1980s.

In February 1994 Washington lifted its nineteen-year economic embargo against Vietnam, and in July 1995 the two countries restored diplomatic relations. Vietnam became the seventh member of ASEAN (Association of South East Asian Nations) in the same month.

Captions to following pages

Pages 184/185: In the port of Haiphong in the Red River delta. Vietnam.

After the wars

The bombing of Haiphong on 23 November 1946 triggered the decisive Vietminh resistance against the colonial administration and was the beginning of the end of French domination in Indochina.

After the American aircraft carrier *Maddox*, which had entered North Vietnamese territorial waters in the Bay of Haiphong, was fired at on 2 August 1964 by North Vietnamese coastguard vessels, the Gulf of Tonkin Resolution was passed. President Johnson used this to justify the escalation of the war.

During the Paris peace negotiations in 1972 President Nixon lifted the restrictions on the bombardment of power stations, docks and shipyards in Haiphong and announced that the harbour was being mined in order to force concessions from Le Duc Tho, the North Vietnamese negotiator.

30,000 tonnes of aid from the Soviet Union and other Communist countries were unloaded in the port daily after the end of the war, while in the eighties, when the harvest in North and Central Vietnam was destroyed by typhoons, so was rice from the Mekong.

To keep pace with the country's predicted economic development, Haiphong's harbour is to be modernized by the end of 1997, with 40 million dollars of Japanese aid.

Japan's huge investment in Vietnam is prompted by fear that Vietnam will emerge unchecked as a new economic force on the Pacific rim. Because of the American embargo, only lifted in 1995, Vietnam was for too long dependent on its Northeast Asian trading partners.

The reopening of the crossing to China at Lang Son in 1989 – ten years after the border war between the former allies Vietnam and China – and the resumption of the rail link between Hanoi and Nanning in 1996 were signs of rapprochement but not complete political normalization between Vietnam and the People's Republic of China. Haiphong is still a strategic port, whether in a conflict over the suspected oil on Paracel and Spratly Islands or over the export of Laotian woods and raw materials.

Page 186: Blind musician on the ferry to Vinh Long. Mekong delta, Vietnam.

Pages 188/189: Aground. On board ship between Myaungmya and Wakema. Irrawaddy, Burma.

Where the sea joins the river

The ships' steersmen on the Irrawaddy know every curve, every fork and bend in the tangle of waterways behind Rangoon. At night they control the great steering wheels with their feet and swing the ship's lights from one palm-covered bank to the other.

The closer the routes are to the sea, the greater the danger of sandbanks. Any delay caused by fog or the transshipment of goods brings the schedule into conflict with the tides. Ships that have run aground stay leaning to one side in the mud in the heat of the day until the tide comes in again.

Pages 190/191: Sandwip islanders catching the ferry to the mainland. Bangladesh.

No firm ground

In the Sandwip Channel, northward-flowing bodies of water from the Bay of Bengal push against the tides of the Ganges and Brahmaputra, carried to sea by the Meghna.

Monsoons, tornadoes and the five-and-a-half metre difference in tide levels make this a particularly dangerous place. In the frequent shipwrecks there are few victims left to be rescued; fishermen and ferry passengers are swept away by the strong current.

Here the gulf is muddied by the river water which has carried down soil from Tibet and Qinghai. The sediments drift out until they are close to the equator and are deposited as deep-sea fans on the sea bed. The sea bed is barely 10,000 years old. And underneath it the Indo-Australian and Southeast Asian shelves – two fragments of the great primordial continent – rub against each other.

Above: A *tokai* with his finds. Dhaka, Bangladesh.

Ali, the son of a rickshaw driver, is eight and the second eldest of six children. The family lives near the Jatrabani dump on the arterial road to Chittagong harbour. On a good day Ali collects five or six sacks of unsorted materials – light bulbs, wire, bottle tops, batteries.

Depending on what he collects, the dealers pay the *tokai* 5 to 20 takas (by way of comparison, a kilo of potatoes costs 5 takas, a kilo of rice 9 takas). The dealers then re-sell bones to mills and they are ultimately bought by Japanese pharmaceutical factories.

On the road in Deltopolis

80,000 rickshaws are officially registered in Dhaka – the number actually estimated to be on the road is 300,000.

Rickshaws are banned from the centre of Ho Chi Minh City, because they hold up the fast-increasing motorcycle and car traffic.

Use of the mobile phone is growing in Bangkok as the time spent in traffic jams increases.

Only 6 per cent of Calcutta consists of streets, whereas the average in cities is 20 per cent. 60 per cent of Calcutta's population suffer from respiratory diseases. The Howrah bridge across the Hooghly, built in 1943, is the busiest bridge in the world, used by 50,000 motor vehicles and a million pedestrians daily. Work has been in progress on Calcutta's underground, the first in South Asia, since 1972.

Since 1991 Shanghai has sunk one centimetre per year under the weight of the biggest building boom in the world; building has more than doubled since 1986.

Above: Knife-grinder on Chittaranjan Avenue. Calcutta, West Bengal, India.

Above right: Morning traffic along the floating market on Ben Nghe canal. Ho Chi Minh City, Vietnam.

Opposite: Rickshaws in the monsoon. Dhaka, Bangladesh.

Acknowledgments

The photographs for this book were taken between May 1991 and February 1995.

Them Thi Truong, born on the Mekong in 1901, showed the way.

The author extends his thanks to:

The editorial staff of the periodical *du* and of the newspaper supplements 'Das Magazin' (*Tages Anzeiger*) and 'Wochenende' (*Neue Zürcher Zeitung*).

The photographers and journalists:
Parveen Anwar, Manuel Bauer, Greg Davis, Craig Fuiji, Philip Jones Griffiths, Morton Hvaal, Bernard Imhasly, Jutta Lietsch, Bertil Lintner, Osman Gani Mansur, Rasul Noorani, Tim Page, Pavel Rahman, Usha Rai, Mohamed Roushanuzzaman, William Shawcross, Peter Sidler, Martin Smith and Richard Vogel. Their patience along the way and the readiness with which they shared their experiences and stories were crucial.

David P. Chandler, Doug Niven and Chris Riley, who let me accompany their Tuol Sleng project.

Albert Lutz of the Museum Rietberg, Zurich, for the invitation to follow in the footsteps of the 17th-century Chinese painter-monk Xiao Yuncong.

The following organizations and government departments for their logistical help:
Associated Press (Dhaka), Bangladesh Red Crescent Society / Cyclone Preparedness Programme (Chittagong), Bangladesh Water Development Board (Chittagong and Khulna), Swiss Agency for Development and Cooperation (Berne and Dhaka), Drik Picture Library (Dhaka), Gono Shahajjo Sangstha (Dhaka), Halo Trust (Cambodia), International Rice Research Institute / University of Cantho (Cantho), IKRK (Phnom Penh), Mekong River Commission (Bangkok), Ministry of Forestry (Dhaka and Khulna), Ministry of Information (Hanoi and Ho Chi Minh City), Ministry of Information (Phnom Penh), Ministry of Irrigation, Water Development and Flood Control (Dhaka), Ministry of Relief and Rehabilitation (Dhaka), Terre des Hommes – Netherland (Dhaka), UNICEF (Dhaka, Rangoon and Zurich), UNHCR (Geneva, Bangkok, Bangladesh and Cambodia), United News of Bangladesh (Dhaka).

The Musée de l'Elysée, Lausanne, and the Kantonales Kuratorium für Kulturförderung, Solothurn, for project contributions in the years 1991 and 1992.

Ilford-Anitec, Fribourg. The author used Ilfobrom Galerie FB photographic paper.

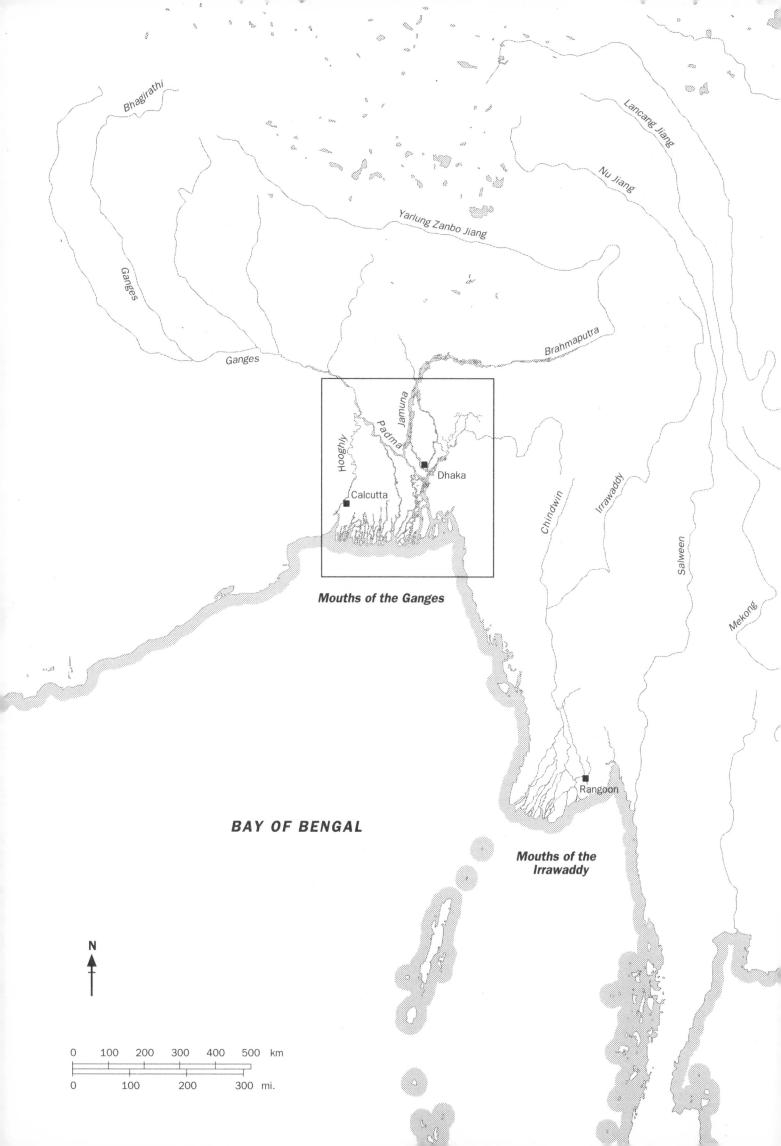

Bhagirathi

Ganges

Lancang Jiang

Nu Jiang

Yarlung Zanbo Jiang

Ganges

Ganges

Brahmaputra

Jamuna

Padma

Hooghly

Dhaka

Calcutta

Chindwin

Irrawaddy

Salween

Mekong

Mouths of the Ganges

Rangoon

BAY OF BENGAL

Mouths of the Irrawaddy

N

0   100   200   300   400   500   km

0   100   200   300   mi.